Life Hikes

Life Hikes

WALKING THROUGH LOSS TO WHAT COMES AFTER

Renée Brown Harmon, MD

MANY HATS
PUBLISHING

Copyright © 2025 by Renée Brown Harmon

All rights reserved.

No part of this book may be reproduced, or stored in a retrieval system, or transmitted in any form or by any means, electronic, mechanical, photocopying, recording, or otherwise, without express written permission of the publisher.

Without in any way limiting the author's and publisher's exclusive rights under copyright, any use of this publication to "train" generative artificial intelligence (AI) technologies to generate text is expressly prohibited. The author reserves all rights to license uses of this work for generative AI training and development of machine learning language models.

Some names and identifying details have been changed to protect the privacy of individuals.

Published by Many Hats Publishing, Birmingham, Alabama
www.reneeharmon.com

Edited and designed by Girl Friday Productions
www.girlfridayproductions.com

Cover design: Emily Weigel and Paul Barrett
Project management: Sara Spees Addicott
Editorial production: Reshma Kooner

Image credits: Cover © Shutterstock/USHENG HSU

ISBN (paperback): 978-1-7347917-3-0
ISBN (ebook): 978-1-7347917-4-7
ISBN (audiobook): 978-1-7347917-5-4

Library of Congress Control Number: 2025918304

First edition

For Elena and Christina.
May you walk home to yourselves every day.

"I go to nature to be soothed and healed, and to have my senses put in order."

—John Burroughs

Contents

Introduction: The Hills Are Alive 1

PART ONE: BEGINNING AGAIN

Beckoning. 13
Chapter 1: The Adventure of Life's Journey 15
Chapter 2: Perspectives on the Road Ahead 28
Chapter 3: Walking with Community 43

PART TWO: MOVING ONWARD

Alzheimer's Beautiful Scars 59
Chapter 4: Trails and Trials 61
Chapter 5: Time Travel 76
Chapter 6: From Fear to Compassion 91

PART THREE: COMING HOME TO MYSELF

Ordinary Day 107
Chapter 7: Adapting to Change 109
Chapter 8: I Already Have All That I Need 123
Chapter 9: The Freedom to Live 138

Conclusion: The Mountains We Climb 152
Acknowledgments 159
Resources 161
About the Author 165

INTRODUCTION

The Hills Are Alive

Eighteen months after my husband's death, four months after retiring from the practice of family medicine, and two months into the Covid lockdown, I was feeling the need to get away from the quiet of my house and the chatter of my own mind. To solve that problem, I decided on a solo trip to the mountains. I would drive my Miata into the forest on the curving mountain roads and find some trails to hike. It would be an adventure, one safe from viral exposure.

As I ascended the road higher and higher, the trees changed from spring's full foliage to bare limbed. It was mid-May, and at the base of the mountains, the deciduous trees' branches were decked in their full early summer garb. As I gained altitude, I noticed that the trees' leaves were now a beautiful spring green. Higher yet, they were just beginning to leaf out, with only the tips of leaves and buds showing. At five thousand feet or more, the trees sported only their winter-bare branches. The temperature declined as I rose, going from summer's warmth to winter's chill in a matter of minutes.

It was fascinating to experience this gradual rolling back of the seasons, the promise of spring always present because I was approaching it or I had just passed through it. At the wintry peak, the images of spring and summer were still fresh in my mind. I had traveled backward through six months' worth of time. It happened so quickly that it almost felt as if I were seeing and living in all those seasons simultaneously.

I had plotted out my course each day, deciding which roads to experience and which hikes to take. The first day's foray took me deep into the forest, along fabulous twisting roads to a trailhead at five thousand feet elevation. It was drizzling and chilly. Due to the dense fog, there was absolutely no view of the meadow and mountains promised by the trail's description. Not the best hike I had taken, but it was wonderful to be outside in the silence of the woods.

The next day, I decided on another hike to a different meadow destination, also at five thousand feet. I put the top down on my convertible because the late afternoon was clear and cool and glorious!

The trail led uphill through a forest full of birdsong, tiny spring flowers, budding trees, and a running stream. The hill crested at a meadow where I encountered a young family taking a trailside blueberry break. Employing social distancing, I skirted around them as we chatted about the beautiful day. It felt so good to interact with these people, however brief it was, because of the isolation in which we had all been living. As I continued through the meadow humming with bees, I had to suppress the urge to break into song. I was that happy, and it was that gorgeous!

The path led through another thicket of woods, uphill again to a second expansive grassy knoll that overlooked a panoramic view of the mountains. I could no longer repress the urge to channel Maria von Trapp. Flinging my arms wide, I twirled and sang in delight the first line of the song "The Sound of Music."

I made my way back down the trail, passed the family again, and stopped to take a photo of the first meadow. As the parking area came into view, I reached into my pocket for my key fob. It was gone.

My mind whirled with the noise of my thoughts. *My key must have fallen out onto the trail but my pocket was zipped up and how will I find it and if I can't find it I will have to call AAA but there is no cell coverage except at the top of this mountain and it's late afternoon so AAA and a locksmith probably can't get to me before nightfall and I can't even wait inside my car because I'm locked out and I will freeze to death or be eaten by a hungry bear or bitten by a rabid dog.*

I climbed back up the mountain, trying to still my swirling brain by methodically scanning the ground for my key fob. I got to the top of the second forested area and met the family again.

"Oh, looks like you're getting good exercise today!" said the dad.

"Actually, I lost my car's key fob, and I'm not having any luck finding it on this rocky and grassy trail."

"What does it look like? I saw a flat black plastic thing lying in the grass."

"That's it! It's my key fob. Did you pick it up?"

"No, but I know exactly where I saw it."

I followed the family down the hill and stopped with them at the spot where I had previously pulled my phone out of my pocket in order to take the photo of the meadow. The dad looked down, picked up an object, and asked, "Is this it?"

"Yes! Oh, my goodness! Thank you!"

"Glad to help. Have a good rest of your day."

"Thank you again. And you too."

And to the children, I whispered, "Your dad is a superhero."

I skipped and whistled all the way back to my car as the last of the day's sunlight drained from the sky.

The kindness of strangers never felt so good as it did right then. As a widow who was recently retired and who had been almost completely isolated for two months, I was not used to interacting with people, and had forgotten how connected we are to one another. We are all family. We need each other.

In gratitude, I breathed in deeply of the mountain air, then placed a small yellow flower on the windshield of the family's car.

HOW DID I END UP HERE?

In my life I have traveled to Greece with a study group, introduced my family to Charleston, South Carolina, where my husband and I did our residencies in family medicine together, and ventured to the Galápagos with my father. I've done solo hiking trips in the southern Appalachian Mountains, an all-women's trek in the Alps, and a climb to the summit of Mount Kilimanjaro. When I plan a trip, I might have a specific plan in mind with a detailed itinerary. There are also the unexpected journeys when I feel untethered to a plan. I may have a vague idea of where I want to go, maybe the beach, but once I'm there, I follow my instincts to rest, play, eat, or exercise when I want. Discovering a new city or area in this way can be rewarding because I have no preconceived notions. The more exciting trips have begun with an unexpected window opening, an opportunity to travel to a place I might not have had on my radar, but something about the view out of that open window calls to me, and I jump at the chance to go.

Travel plans can go off the rails too. Weather might force a change of plans. I've experienced an airline flight delay that cut short a long-planned vacation, and I've had to spend an unexpected night in an airport hotel instead of completing my journey home. Never have I planned an excursion and ended up in an entirely different location.

But life can do just that. We can plan our path forward in life, making all the right decisions to meet our goals, relying on the app of life: our internal compass, outside guidance, and our intellect. But unexpected obstacles and blessings will arise. We can't anticipate everything, even if we have calculated all the pros and cons of a course of action. All the planning in the world can't predict an automobile accident, an unfaithful spouse, a once-in-a-century flood, a bad investment, an unexpected diagnosis.

This is a lesson I learned firsthand when my husband, Harvey, a fifty-year-old doctor who loved marathons, family vacations to national parks, and our long line of family dogs, was diagnosed with younger-onset Alzheimer's disease in 2010.

You can rely on a map when curveballs come up while traveling. There is comfort in knowing where you are in the world, where you are going, what you might see along the way, or how you might troubleshoot issues. Whether a paper map, GPS, guidebook, or itinerary, these resources help us when traveling in unknown territory. But life doesn't offer a map. After Harvey's diagnosis, I desperately wanted someone to tell us exactly what we could expect along the way, a guidebook of sorts. We were told that younger-onset Alzheimer's disease is exactly like the Alzheimer's disease of old age. It has the same symptoms and time frame—the same trajectory—but it is defined by a diagnosis occurring before the age of sixty-five. A detailed guidebook for Alzheimer's disease just isn't possible. It felt as if we were given the diagnosis then told "Good luck. See you in six months."

My memoir, *Surfing the Waves of Alzheimer's: Principles*

of Caregiving That Kept Me Upright, details that journey. In it, I share how I experienced the initial jolt of fear that something was wrong with Harvey's cognition while on a family vacation, and how I navigated getting a diagnosis—including calling our state medical licensing board looking for guidance in how to address his desire to continue practicing medicine. It chronicles the four years that Harvey was able to be home alone, the two years when I employed caregivers to be with him, and the two years he spent in memory care and geriatric psychiatry units. The memoir ends with his death from aspiration pneumonia in October 2018. Those eight years were difficult, especially without a map. I managed by trusting my own inner strength, by relying on loving family and friends, by immersing myself in nature when possible. And mostly, by seeking ways to interact with love and effectiveness with my husband.

While I talk about Harvey a lot in this book, it isn't meant to be another memoir of my experience through his illness and death. Instead, this book shares lessons from my experiences while hiking, observing nature, and traveling. My hope is that readers will develop new ways of knowing how we as humans and caregivers—whether to children, aging parents, spouses, friends, the environment, or in our line of work—might think about life's challenges in new ways and learn to live more authentically and abundantly.

We all experience challenges throughout our lives, some expected—the births of our children, the deaths of aged relatives—and some totally unexpected. My life together with Harvey felt charmed before his diagnosis. We shared a family medicine practice in a suburb of Birmingham, Alabama, from 1992 until he was forced to retire in 2010 because of his diagnosis. We also shared responsibilities at home, raising our two daughters, Elena and Christina, and managing the household. Our unique model of alternating days at home with days at the office afforded us both the time and space to be equally involved in both spheres.

Once Harvey retired, not only did I become his primary caregiver, but I also became a full-time solo medical practitioner, chief executive officer and chief financial officer at the office and at home, and primary parent to two teenage daughters. There was a lot to manage—so many hats, so many plates in the air.

I retired from the practice of medicine in 2019, about a year after Harvey died and just before the Covid epidemic hit. A lot of those first few years were spent writing my memoir and getting it published and out into the world. After the pandemic eased a bit, I started speaking and giving presentations to groups of caregivers, sharing our family's story with Alzheimer's disease. Meeting fellow caregivers in the midst of their journey and offering some of what I had learned was life-giving to me and was well received.

Travel had always been a big part of my life, and since I couldn't do that during Covid, hiking was my saving grace during those months of isolation. I couldn't go far, but I ranged away from home in my car, using my hiking app and paper maps in search of new trails. I started to find that, while grief was always with me in some way, nothing lifted me out of it quite like when I was moving my feet, especially in a forest. As we settled into a new normal, I began traveling again—sometimes alone, sometimes with Elena and Christina (now grown) and their guys.

And I wrote, building up this collection of essays. They are not all nature or travel related, and they certainly are not all related to caregiving and grief, though those themes percolate throughout. Though not overtly spiritual, the Divine shows up throughout, as the Divine tends to do.

I was raised in a traditional Protestant home, and I now consider myself a progressive Christian. As I have grown and experienced more of the world, I have come to respect and treasure different worldviews regarding religion and the realms of spirituality. I no longer believe in my childhood image of God as an old man sitting on a throne on a cloud, directing the weather, ordering our lives, or smiting unbelievers. God is love. That's the crux of my belief system. That's all that really matters. And if God is love, then God loves all of humanity and all of creation. And we are called to do the same.

The word *God* carries some baggage for me and for many. It conjures that bearded old man of my childhood. Because I now believe that God is genderless, I also prefer to use terms that are more inclusive of my understanding of God as love. So I tend to use *the Divine*, *Spirit*, or *the Universe*, where others might use *God*.

Another aspect of spirituality that resonates with me is the belief that God lives within each of us. A bit of divinity is in each of our souls, and when we are living into our souls, that bit of divinity shines more brightly. Therefore, I tend to use the term *god-spark* when I speak of that better nature of our being.

My hope is that if you are suffering from life's slings and arrows, opening the pages of this book might offer a modicum of relief as well as a new way to look at your particular journey of life. Or at least a moment of feeling as if you are not alone. We are all in this together. We are all family on this wonder-full, spinning green-and-blue planet. We will get from here to there, with or without a map, by relying on the god-spark within and on the blessing of community. They will show us the way forward.

To more literally get from here to there, I've driven and ridden in cars of all shapes and sizes, buses, motorcycles, and bicycles—over paved or gravel roads, highways, and interstates. I've ridden trains on this continent and in Europe. I've paddled canoes, kayaks, surfboards, and paddleboards on rivers, lakes, and oceans. I've voyaged in inflatable rafts, sport boats, cruise ships, and sailboats. I've flown in airplanes and helicopters across the country and across the Atlantic. I've even "flown" on a tandem hang glider, a parasail, and a zip line.

These modes of transportation can parallel different portions of my life. Sometimes I zip along a freeway, breezing through my life. Other times, I have to paddle hard against a prevailing current. At certain times in my life, like an airplane trip, I arrive at a distant location in an unexpectedly short time. Often, I drive solo, but other times I am joined by a community of travelers. Some trips and life journeys are exhilarating, and others offer the space to move at a leisurely pace.

However you get where you're going, at whatever pace or timing, remember that it isn't always about the destination. After all, the end of the line for all of us will be the same. No matter where we go or what we do, we all have a finite time on earth. It may be a cliché, but life is about the journey, and I'd like to thank you for walking with me for part of it.

PART ONE

Beginning Again

BECKONING

The mountain is whispering,
Come and dance.
Her voice speaks of crystal air, and
Sheer walls of rock, tipped in snow.
She beckons with the
Wide-open arms of her horizons.
She invites a flinging of my own,
Spinning, an untethering.

Come. Stretch out your soul. Dance.

Or else
She whispers a dance of stillness,
Raise your arms, child, she says.
Allow the umbilical cord of your body
To connect heaven with earth,
Clouds with dirt.

I used to be a dancing girl.
Sneakers, stilettos, sensible flats
Replaced the dancing shoes

Hanging on the wall of memory.
But the mountain calls me to dance again.

No more shimmying up to the idea of the
    dance,
Eyes averted, as if asking not to be seen.
No more tap dancing around the fact that
This girl-woman still wants to dance.
No more painful dancing in pointe shoes,
Molding my life-dance into perfection.

This is modern dance—
Free-form twists and glides and swoops,
Listening to my body, my life,
And moving in ways that liberate.

And when I finish my dance with the
    mountain,
There will be no applause, no curtain call.
The stones, grass, sky, birds, blooms
Are audience enough.

There is no need for this dancing woman
To hang up her shoes again.
The dance of my life will continue—
On the hills, on the plains, on the rivers
    and oceans.

But first, the mountain.

She is whispering.

CHAPTER 1

The Adventure of Life's Journey

None of the means of transportation could get me to the other side of grief quite as well as my feet. Not that one ever gets to the other side of grief. It is always there, and always will be. Its size and shape may change over time, but my heart will always have a hole in it for Harvey. That hole is filled with love, and that will never change.

Hiking was a natural and easy activity for Harvey and me to continue to enjoy together when he was living with Alzheimer's disease. Being diagnosed at the age of fifty, he was still very fit and active, even running marathons in the first two years of his diagnosis. As the disease progressed, and he was unable to go on walks or runs by himself without getting lost, we would walk together in the early mornings and hike on the weekends. We didn't need words or communication to walk the paths. We could just be together, experiencing the natural world around us—listening, looking, and smelling.

As the disease progressed further, and Harvey was less

and less physically able to walk safely, I continued to hike on my own, mostly solo. I also began to travel alone, seeking out trails wherever I went. There was something intrinsically healing about being alone, surrounded by forest, my thoughts ranging freely. I could release my anxiety and sadness about Harvey's decline and just "be." Occasionally, one or both of my daughters would accompany me on my ramblings, and we would talk or not, healing together in shared silence.

After Harvey passed away, I continued my solo sojourns, my feet logging miles in forests near and far, taking me closer to my center, my true self, the Divine god-spark within. I know most of the area trails really well, having hiked them many times. But I continue to be surprised by details I see on a path—a large blue flat-topped mushroom, a turtle right in the middle of the trail, tiny toads hopping across my way, new-to-me wildflowers, a flurry of butterflies as I crossed a footbridge, a fat black snake draped over the railing of a bridge. These moments don't happen on every hike, but often enough that I continue to traverse the same trails, always on the lookout for something fresh.

Hiking is sometimes just a walk in the woods. But just as there are different types of surfaces on which my car travels, there are different types of trails, each having their unique set of advantages and disadvantages. If I want to hike for pure exercise, getting my heart rate up, I will choose a wide, flat trail, and book it at a fast pace, maybe even doing a little trail-running. There's nothing that can trip me up, nothing unexpected. If I want a more intense workout, I will find a long trail with a significant incline to challenge myself. If I want to slow down and pay attention, I will choose a hilly single-track path. These are my favorites.

These narrow trails can be more treacherous—rocky or rooty, slick with mud, or steep and requiring long stretches of my legs. I can't always anticipate what I will encounter, and what seems like an easy trail can turn out to be hazardous. I once fell flat on my butt when standing facing downhill on a slight incline of pea gravel. I had shifted my weight ever so slightly, and because my shoes didn't have the best traction, my feet just flew up in front of me, and down I went.

If I plan my hike using my hiking app and reading reviews, I feel prepared for what I might encounter along the trail. Of course, there are always surprises. The app isn't always up to date. There have been a few hikes that took me by surprise, as they weren't described accurately on the app. I've gotten in over my head just a few times, and luckily I knew enough to make my way back to the trailhead before disaster hit. All my planning also can't prepare me for unexpected obstacles. That's part of the excitement—not knowing exactly what I will find, even if it's a trail I've hiked before. And, of course, unexpected beautiful plants and vistas or encounters with wildlife are part of what makes being in nature magical.

Life, like hiking, can do just that too. You make all the proper decisions about how you envision your life to be going forward only to have those plans slip sideways. My life's course certainly became an unexpected path with Harvey's diagnosis. I was so proud of the life we had built together, sharing responsibilities at home as well as at our family medicine clinic that we had built from scratch. But almost as soon as my alarm bells went off about his cognitive problems, I began to grieve, before he even had an official diagnosis. If my gut was right, and the diagnosis I feared most was correct, our life together was about to be dramatically altered. I was going to be in for a world of pain and grief for many years.

GRIEF ISN'T LINEAR

I was well aware of Dr. Elisabeth Kübler-Ross's five stages of grief, defined in 1969: denial, anger, bargaining, depression, and acceptance. Designed to describe what a person diagnosed with a terminal illness may experience, these stages over time have come to reflect grief more broadly—including illness, divorce, and job loss—not only for those suffering a personal loss but also for their friends and family. Dr. Kübler-Ross did not intend to suggest that a person moves through these stages one at a time. More often, each stage makes their appearance sporadically, and sometimes together.

I wish grief was a clear-cut, linear process that led straight to acceptance on a set timeline. It would make it so much easier if grief followed a simple progression that everyone experienced in the same way. But, no, like most of life, grief is more complex than a clearly defined five-step process. Throw dementia into the mix, and grief really gets complicated. I experienced every one of Dr. Kübler-Ross's stages during Harvey's time with dementia, sometimes cycling through them all in a single day.

- Denial: "Maybe it's not as bad as I imagine it. Maybe it was just an ordinary middle-aged brain slip."
- Anger: "Why is this happening to us?! It's not fair! He did everything right!"
- Bargaining: "Please don't let this disease be hereditary. Let it be me instead of our daughters."
- Depression: "I just can't do it anymore. I give up."
- Acceptance: "All right. I am strong. We can get through this, relying on the love I have for Harvey and our daughters. I will do whatever I need to do to keep him safe and content."

While the sorrow and grief began before Harvey's diagnosis, it lasted for the eight years that he lived with Alzheimer's disease, and after he passed away. I had to learn how to cope with my grief for a very long time. With the distance of time and the perspective of hindsight, I have come to recognize how grief was, is, and will be an integral part of my life.

When I looked up "types of grief," the internet offered up a plethora of articles. I found one that described eighteen different types of grief. So much grief! What follows are the ones that were, and sometimes continue to be, a part of my grief process.

Anticipatory grief is experienced by those who are diagnosed with a terminal illness, as well as their loved ones. As the name implies, anticipatory grief entails looking ahead to a known, certain, future death. For a diagnosis of Alzheimer's disease, this grief can last long years.

I grieved for our past, all of the present moments as they passed, and the future. When I looked back at the beginning of our relationship, and our years forming our medical practice and starting our family, it was with a mix of love and sadness. Such youth and lightheartedness. Such confidence and expectancy. In looking back with nostalgia, there is a sense of loss of what was. I grieved with each present moment as they arrived—each new loss of an ability, each indicator that he was worsening, each milestone he missed in our daughters' lives. I grieved most for the loss of our future plans—travel, retirement, moving to a new location, and new experiences we would have. I grieved for all the moments he would not experience—our daughters' graduations, weddings, and the births of grandchildren. I grieved hard for our daughters and what they would miss as well as grieving that they would have to help care for their father.

Another form, *ambiguous loss*, as described by Dr. Pauline Boss, is a type of grief that applies to situations when a physical body cannot be recovered. It can also apply to a psychological loss, which is when the physical body is still there, but the person is psychologically absent. Harvey's body was present, but the personality that I had known and loved for over thirty years was disappearing. It was impossible to gain closure, constantly assessing and enumerating new losses, and grieving them, all while my husband was still alive. He was there, but not there. My memories of who Harvey used to be were clouded by who he was in that present moment. And he continued to change, so that I was constantly grieving the persons he had been, remembering all his past incarnations. I felt validated by being able to name this type of loss and grief I was experiencing because it was so, well, ambiguous.

Disenfranchised grief also reared its ugly head. I encountered this when it felt as if my grief was discounted. "How can you be grieving when he's still alive?" "At least you still have him," "At least he still knows you," and all the other "at leasts." Sometimes even well-intentioned comments can discount your reality. "But he looks so good!" people might say, leaving me with a pit in my stomach. Even "It looks like he's having a good day today" felt like a slap to the face when I was living every day with loss and grief.

Then there's the grief that comes with the loss of the role of caregiver, when you're feeling adrift without that role. "Who am I now if I am not a caregiver?" "How do I structure my now shapeless days?" Even when there is relief that the suffering is over, the loss of that sense of self can be staggering as we struggle to figure out "what's next?"

WRITING IT OUT

I mostly filled the void I felt after Harvey passed away by continuing to journal and to hike. I had been journaling throughout Harvey's time with Alzheimer's disease, pouring out all my doubts, fears, anger, anxiety, and deep, deep sadness, filling six notebooks. My journal was a safe place to spew all that I was feeling as well as my cries of lament. I could work through my emotional landscape by writing it out, then rereading it if I wanted to see where I was on this journey of grief.

Within those pages, I grieved each slow, incremental loss that Harvey sustained as he regressed further and further from the man I had known him to be. Harvey gradually lost the ability to converse, then to speak at all. He forgot how to cook his favorite recipes. He couldn't remember how to do the laundry, then drive a car, or eventually even how to feed the dog.

But it was also through those pages that I was able to create my memoir, and writing that book was as therapeutic as the journaling. By having a project as daunting as writing and publishing a book, I kept my mind occupied. Realizing that the book would have an impact on others affected by Alzheimer's disease and other dementias was humbling and empowering. I started writing a weekly blog about dementia and speaking to caregiving groups. Telling our story was healing me, and it had the potential to heal others.

So journaling was a major source of my healing. I knew that journaling was good for my soul, and I have recognized it as part of my own self-care. Now it is scientifically proven that journaling is beneficial in multiple aspects of health.

The benefits come from writing about your experiences and the emotions provoked by them—expressive writing. Journaling, beyond giving an account of your day, is a way of processing your feelings about those events. This serves to create an understandable narrative, and to reduce your stress by confronting unpleasant emotions. The intensity of difficult emotions lessens over time as they become more understandable and fit within a story. The more often you encounter the stressful situation in your journaling, the less intense the emotions become—exposure therapy. This has proven to be a helpful adjunct to psychotherapy for patients living with post-traumatic stress disorder (PTSD), so I surmise that it would also work in processing all types of grief, stress, and trauma.

There are also scientific studies that point to some other mental health benefits of journaling. I imagine most of us who have provided care for a loved one with memory deficits wonder if and when we ourselves might be affected. You can imagine the comfort I felt when I read that journaling has been proven to improve memory. Writing about our stresses expressively frees up our brains so that our working memory—which helps with decision-making and behavior—has greater capacity. When we are not overly occupied with the hardships, having worked through them on paper, we can use our brains more effectively in everyday situations. In addition, research has shown that writing things down improves our memories by more deeply encoding them in our brains. I can attest to this. When I began writing my memoir, I rarely referred to the journals I kept during Harvey's illness except to verify dates. Because I had written out most of the stories already, the memories were readily available to me.

Research also shows that journaling in longhand has advantages over typing on the computer. More parts of the brain are utilized, and the practice is better for mindfulness, generating ideas, and working through emotions, because it's a slower process. Living only in your head and your heart can be taxing. By using your body, you may achieve more balance and wholeness in your life as a human in this world.

It was only after my memoir was published that I learned about David Kessler's work on a final, sixth stage of grief—*finding meaning*. It was a light bulb moment: That's exactly what I was doing by writing and speaking! I was creating meaning from our painful eight-year journey. But it's not necessary to write a book, become an activist, or start a nonprofit in order to create meaning from loss. The best definition of this sixth stage that I've found is this: It is when you can remember your loved one with more love than sorrow.

I want to acknowledge grief in all its facets, but I don't want it to end there. Deep grief also means there was once great love. Grief is a kind of love, and by remembering that this is a type of love, there can be healing.

EMBRACE THE UNEXPECTED

It was a nice afternoon at the beach, if a bit cool. With temperatures hovering around fifty-five degrees, I decided to brave it. I reasoned that if I kept low enough to the ground, the chilly wind wouldn't find me. The sky was cloudless, so surely the sunshine would warm me.

I like to head to one of my favorite Florida Panhandle beaches by myself sometime after Christmas and New Year's—an escape after the holiday frenzy. The rates and crowds are at their lowest, and the weather is always warmer than it is in my hometown of Birmingham, Alabama, even if it's not quite balmy. It's hit or miss. Some winters, the temperature has hit seventy degrees.

This day was quite pleasant, so, donning my lightweight puffer coat over leggings and a long-sleeved top, I carried my bag of supplies to the beach—minus my beach chair, which I'd left at home. Inhaling the tang of the ocean, I spread out my smallish towel and took off my coat, socks, and shoes. Then I settled onto my back, wiggling my butt from side to side to contour the underlying sand to my backside. I held my new read, a paperback novel recommended by my sister, in front of my face to block the sun. Soon, I was absorbed in the perfect beach read—quick, easy, and fun.

When my back began to ache a bit from lying in this position, I turned over to my stomach. This was no easy feat for me, a woman in her early sixties, on the sand, but with a few grunts, I managed to lift my butt and hoist it up and over without flinging too much sand. I propped myself up on my elbows, my puffer coat now supporting my chest. I read on.

Chomp!

I felt something lightly clamp down on my right foot, at the instep. I squealed, and with lots of sand flying, rolled over and abruptly sat up. I was eye to eye with a brown pelican. Its beak was open, and I could see the blunt sawtooth-ridged edge running down the length of both the top and bottom bills, the pouch hanging loosely. We eyed each other warily. Well, I was wary. Evidently, the bird was hungry. It wasn't belligerent or aggressive, just curious. I guess my foot's livid pinkish-gray coloration, in contrast with my black leggings, presented the apparition of a fish. A pelican tried to eat my foot!

A young couple walked up, asking if I was OK. Evidently, they had been following the pelican as it ambled down the beach. They saw it head toward me and wondered if it would try to get into my beach bag, looking for food. They said that they didn't want to startle me by calling out. So the pelican startled me by biting down on my foot instead! The couple tried to chase it off for me, and then they kept walking down the beach.

But the bird stayed. I was no longer interested in my novel. I had to keep watch over the pest of a pelican. Looking at me out of the corner of its eye, it continued to stare at my foot. What was so enticing about my foot? I tried to shoo it away, but it would only scamper away a few yards before circling back, sidling closer, eyeing me sideways. Eventually, it flew away, landing on the water, and bobbed on the surface of the ocean.

This was the strangest, most bizarre wildlife encounter I have ever had. I didn't know what to make of it. It made no sense, yet it happened. It did no damage to my foot at all. No blood was drawn, no tooth or beak marks were made. If I were alone and the couple had not witnessed the aborted feast, no one would believe me. I took a picture of the bird, but it's no proof that this event really happened.

Inexplicable things happen. We find ourselves on an unexpected path of life, one we never had imagined, wondering how we came to be on this particular road. We can try to decipher meaning or make sense of it, but in the end, we just have to accept it. A bizarre diagnosis, a stunning coincidence, an unexplainable event—there are mysteries that leave us in wonder, confusion, or dismay. I could waste a lot of mental energy trying to understand why a pelican would try to eat my foot, or why my husband developed Alzheimer's disease. In the end, both events were just mileposts on the adventure of my life's journey.

The shock of feeling the pelican's beak on my foot was also a reminder that grief itself can follow an unexpected path. I was having a perfectly relaxing day on the beach when it was suddenly interrupted—just like when moments of pain over the loss of my husband overtake me for no particular reason. I may think that most of my grief has passed, and it mostly has, then I can be slammed again with its intensity. The frequency and intensity of the pain have both lessened with time, but even today, six years after Harvey died, a memory or song or even someone else's story can put me right back in that feeling.

There is no clear, straight path through the grief process. We each navigate it in our own way and at our own pace. Some people cry easily, others not at all. Some feel the need to talk about their deceased loved one, gaining solace from sharing memories and being supported by their community. Others don't or won't feel comfortable in the company of others and prefer to seek shelter alone. Many couples and families experience this as conflict, each member processing their grief in their individual way and not understanding how those closest to them are not experiencing it in the same manner.

Just days after Harvey died, I was with one of our daughters when grief washed over me, and I dissolved into tears. I laid my head in her lap, longing to be comforted by her. She didn't know what to do. I can imagine that it felt awkward for her, on her own grief journey, to know what to do with her sobbing mother. I felt it as rejection or a discounting of my pain, when in reality, we were each on our own path of grief, and they were not intersecting at that particular moment. It didn't damage our relationship, and we were able to talk through it later, but it was a reminder that we all grieve in our own way.

Walking, and especially hiking, helped me navigate the variable and unexpected path of grief. When I escape into a forest, my mind necessarily pays attention to the trail. It has less space to ruminate on the concerns that might otherwise preoccupy me. When I'm not listening to music or a podcast, my mind can range freely, taking in all that I see, hear, and smell. I have even practiced telling stories or giving presentations while hiking. Just last week, I found myself crafting a fictional story in my mind.

Beyond being a diversion from grief and other concerns, hiking is a reminder that unexpected events are just part of life's journey. Even if I walk the same trail two days in a row, something new or different is bound to appear—rain the night before may bring a crop of mushrooms, or perhaps an indigo bunting makes an appearance. That's part of the pleasure I find—I never know what I'll see.

And just like any of life's challenges, the way forward through grief may include a steep trail, and climbing it requires effort and stamina. At some points, the crest of the incline can't even be seen, and it feels impossible to gain the peak. "When will I ever feel normal again?" At other times, grief appears as a wide, flat, straight, and easily navigable path.

"I've got this." Like an unseen rock, grief can momentarily trip me up. "Wow! Where did that memory come from?" And just like a downed tree across the trail can stop me in my tracks and require a new plan to get around or through it, an episode of grief can overwhelm me from out of the blue. "What do I do now? I thought I was over this grief."

So grieve the way you need to grieve. Don't let anyone try to talk you out of your sadness if that's not where you are on your journey. Well-meaning people in your life may not like to feel your pain up close, and may avoid the subject or even you yourself. Take care of yourself the way you know to be best for you. Perhaps journaling will guide you on your way. Seek out a grief support group if that feels right. Take a walk, with a friend or alone, in your neighborhood or on a nearby trail. Travel through grief and loss your way.

CHAPTER 2

Perspectives on the Road Ahead

I have always loved maps and globes. I have early memories of taking out the maps in my father's *National Geographic* magazines and poring over them. I remember turning the outdated globe in our family den for hours, playing "Where will I be in ten years?" I have my own outdated globe now, and a huge, beautifully detailed topographical map of the world hangs in my study. My glove compartment is filled with state maps that I have collected from welcome stations even though I now mostly rely on GPS. A physical map still gives me a sense of being in control, of knowing where I am, of being able to see the bigger picture, and of being able to plan ahead.

In 2010, the summer before her senior year of high school, and around the time of Harvey's official diagnosis, Harvey and I took a trip with our oldest daughter, Elena, to visit colleges. As the perpetual navigator of the family, I had the route mapped out, a plan for where we would stop for the night, and an idea of how long it would take to get to each destination. I had that glove compartment full of maps, and the GPS would be my backup.

Going north on I-65 toward our first stop, Nashville, I opened the glove box to get out the map. To my horror, there was none. We had taken Harvey's car, and there were no maps in his glove compartment. I calmed down, reasoning that I already knew where we were generally going, and the GPS could guide us to a specific location. It would be fine.

We made it to the first college easily, and as we headed out of Nashville to the second college, I plugged the destination into the GPS. It said we were twelve hours away. This was not right; I had mapped it all out before we left. It was supposed to be a six-hour trip. I decided to trust my prior research and ignore the stupid GPS. If only I had a map. Well, I reasoned, I could do this without a map. It would be fine.

As we closed in on the North Carolina border and its welcome station, however, I knew I had to get a map. I could not stand to be without one. A supplier was just around the corner. I could feed the hole in my soul, fill up the void, and make the anxiety go away with a simple map. I didn't really *need* the map; I just wanted it for the moment. I was doing fine without it.

We stopped at the North Carolina welcome station and got a map. A wave of pure relief washed over me. Aah . . .

Why did I want that map so badly? Why could I not trust my instincts to get us where we were going? I needed to see the big picture and where we fit within it. I needed to see the small details of roads and towns and mileages. What did it say about me that I needed to know where I was, where I had been, and where I was going? How would my life be different if I just traveled the road before me, trusting that I would get to where I was supposed to be?

And then it hit me. This Alzheimer's World that Harvey and I had just entered did not come with a map. The neuropsychologist didn't diagnose my husband, tell him he should not work anymore, and then hand us a guidebook that outlined exactly where we were going. I asked, "What is Harvey's likely course? Where will he be in five years?" The answer I got was "Every person is different. We cannot say."

We were plopped down in the middle of Alzheimer's World without a map, and we would have to navigate the way. I would rather have had a map of the future; I wanted to know where we were and where we were going. I wanted to see the forest and each tree. I wanted to know what we would be seeing along the way and how long it would take us to get from here to there.

In the end, I did develop a map of sorts. I researched. I read. I looked ahead, tentatively, at what the future might hold. I asked myself questions like "How will I know when he should not drive?" and "How will I know when I need more help?" Then I worked out possible answers. I wasn't able to anticipate everything, but it calmed me to think ahead and make a plan, creating a map for myself.

And what were my guideposts? How did I know that we were on the right road and hadn't taken a wrong turn? I relied on my instincts for that—and how Harvey responded. I learned to trust wise friends to point me in a different direction if we were veering off course—if they saw that one or both of us were not coping well. I continued to take care of myself in all the ways I had in the past and looked for new practices as time went on. I created a map that was unique to us.

With that create-as-you-go map, we made our way into Alzheimer's World, navigating the waves and obstacles that presented themselves, as they presented themselves. Sometimes, you just have to look at your world from a different angle—looking back, looking at it from another's point of view, or stepping away and seeing the big picture when all you know is what is directly in front of you, what needs your attention at the moment. Journaling, and then reading over entries, gave me a better perspective of the trail we were traveling.

Our map might not have been the detailed thing of beauty that hangs in my study, but it was one that we created together and was uniquely ours. We might not have had a guidebook, but I had my love for Harvey, my community, and my trust that we would find our way.

FORESTS AND TREES

One autumn, my cousin Anna asked if I could find acorn caps for a craft project she was planning. The only ones she had access to were too small for her plans. She didn't tell me what her project was, but I complied. The water oak in my front yard provides shade for my alfresco dining porch as well as support for a string of lights. The acorns from this oak tree are tiny, likely what Anna had at home, so they wouldn't work. As I planned my neighborhood walk that morning, I decided I would keep my eyes open for acorn caps. The neighborhood is named Forest Park, an apt name for an area of streets lined with mature trees. Surely I would find some suitable oak trees.

After donning a skort with large pockets, I set off. I knew there were no oak trees on the first portion of my walk, so I lifted my head and savored the bright blue skies and crisp fall air. When I reached a section of the neighborhood that was particularly shaded by large deciduous trees, I began to scan the sidewalk in front of me. There were all kinds of autumn detritus on the path—leaves, twigs, ginkgo fruit, and weeds poking through the cracks made by the roots of the big trees. If I really slowed down, I saw an occasional snail or the quick movement of a lizard out of the corner of my eye.

And acorns, with and without their caps, in such variety! I saw lots of the tiny water oak acorns and some medium-sized ones. The treasure was a motherlode of extremely large acorns, some one and a half inches in diameter. I filled my pockets, wondering if anyone was noticing my very odd behavior.

Farther on in my walk I found some very peculiar-looking acorn caps, with frilly offshoots covering them. I vowed I would look up the different species of oaks based on their acorns when I got home. That's when I realized that I had never even looked at the trees themselves—the trunks, the bark, the branches, or the leaves—all the identifying markers of a tree. I've always thought of myself as one who sees a forest for the trees, but here I was not even looking at the trees, much less the forest. I was only looking at what was on the ground, what the trees could provide me—the acorns that the trees had shed.

I believe that the world would be a better place if we saw whole persons and not just what they can provide for us or do for us. We may just see their outer form, but these "acorns" of people's lives are just a small portion of what we see, and that's never all there is to a life. Your mail carrier might have a spouse and children. The woman that checks out your groceries may play in a band on the weekends. The kids crossing your lawn on the way home from school might be on their way to help care for an ailing grandparent.

It's always good to remember that each individual we come in contact with has as full a life as each of us do. We do not know the richness or entirety of others' lives, but we can begin by acknowledging that reality.

The lives of the individuals and families who are affected by Alzheimer's disease, other dementias, or any terminal illness have complete stories, too, from before the diagnosis. It is important to honor their prior lives and not see them as their current selves only. In adult day care, respite care, and memory care units, families are often asked to create a memory box with photos and items from the loved one's past. Some memory care units have a shadow box outside the door of each resident, and the family is asked to fill it with these items. This serves to help the resident identify their room, and it also helps the staff to appreciate who each of their residents is. It can be a point of entry for the staff to reach a resident in conversations and interactions. Using the photos and items in Harvey's memory box, my daughters and I would connect with him on visits, and I always hung his medical diploma in each of his rooms at care facilities.

Persons living with dementia were once engineers, bakers, physicians, homemakers, bankers, and teachers—as well as husbands, wives, sisters, fathers, and friends. They were important people, gentle people, outrageous people, melancholy people, and adventurous people. They were individuals who contributed to their families and their communities.

I have a friend who has compiled two collections of stories into books entitled *Before the Diagnosis*. In it, family and friends tell stories about the remarkable lives of their loved ones who are currently living with, or have succumbed to, some form of dementia. As I was writing my contribution, I was flooded with many precious memories of Harvey—our life together as a young couple, then as new parents, and all our memorable family vacations and holidays.

I was reminded by these memories that the richness of my particular life before Harvey's diagnosis was molded by my need for balance. This was most evident in my professional and family life. Harvey and I, as individuals and as a couple, achieved balance in our work and home lives because it was a priority. Much has been written about the work-life balance, and few are able to attain it, but because Harvey and I valued each other, our careers, and our family in the same manner, we were able to do it. Harvey was unusual in that he didn't have the need to be head of the household, or the primary breadwinner. He viewed me as his equal in all things. For my part,

I knew from early on that I wanted a career that mattered and that I wanted a family. I came of age in the 1970s and 1980s, a time when women were told that we could all be superwomen. And I believed it. I just didn't know how much easier and satisfying it would be if one married a man such as Harvey. That was our story, "before."

Sometimes, conjuring memories of a loved one from before their time with dementia can be painful because it can be a realization of all that has been lost. But when we can focus, with gratitude, on their lives—their love of us, their contributions to their world, and the amazing lives they have led—the heaviness can lift, and our load feels lighter. We are remembering them with more love than sorrow.

We think of funerals as the time to honor those we loved, but we should honor them, too, while they are alive, by sharing stories and memories. And it's important to also honor family caregivers' lives before the diagnosis. They, too, matter. They are more than the title *caregiver*.

Achieving balance as a physician, mother, business owner, and caregiver was important to me. I didn't want to lose sight of who I was, and I didn't want to lose sight of who my husband was. I'm not sure that I succeeded, but I tried because it was the only way I knew to be.

If we can look at others with a different perspective, we can also look through a longer lens to gain a perspective and see that our time on earth is but a brief moment. Maybe our problems don't seem so daunting when viewed through that lens.

ADJUSTING PERSPECTIVE

In the autumn of 2023, I journeyed with a couple of friends to Redwoods National Park. My travel companions and I were chatting amiably when we got out of the car at the small parking area of the trail we had selected. We had already driven through the Avenue of the Giants, mouths agape. Then we had stopped at the visitor center, gathering information about the coast redwoods we had been driving through.

Nothing could have prepared me for entering the forest of gigantic trees on foot, though. My friends and I stopped our conversation in mid-sentence and stood in awe. As I stepped onto the trail, eyes adjusting to the low light, words escaped me. All around me were massive tree trunks. A few had fallen, their root systems exposed. The ground and some of the older fallen trees were carpeted with redwood sorrel, a large clover-like plant, and ferns as high as my waist. I kept imagining that a dinosaur would appear from behind one of the huge trunks. We were silent, and, curiously, the forest was silent as well, save for one crow. We had entered a hushed cathedral, an ancient and holy sanctuary.

The flat, easy trail was only two and a quarter miles long, but it took well over two hours to walk it because we would frequently stop to drink it all in, murmuring, "Oh, my God!" The photos we took could not do the trees justice. Only by taking a photo with a person in it for perspective could we capture a notion of the immensity of these behemoths, but it's impossible to capture the whole experience in a photo.

Earlier in the week, we had visited Muir Woods National Monument near San Francisco and were introduced to the first of these giants. Because the park is so popular, we had to preregister our parking and entrance fees. I soon learned why. There were people everywhere. The trees were there too, of course, and I was struck by their majesty, but being surrounded by humanity, most of whom were conversing loudly, many on their phones, distracted me from fully experiencing the place. Many people ignored the signs asking visitors to be silent on a section of the heavily trafficked path. Only after we left this trail to pick up another did I get a taste of what was to come the next day.

Standing up to 350 feet tall, the coast redwood sports a deeply grooved spongy bark, the grooves up to twelve inches deep. Most patterns of bark are as vertical as the trees, while others spiral upward. This outer covering is home to an untold number of tiny plants and animals, not to mention what resides in the canopy. Looking up, following the arrow-straight trunk high into the canopy was a vertiginous experience. All I could see was a tuft of green.

These trees can live for more than two thousand years, their lifespans making a mockery of our brief sojourns. These giants have borne witness to thousands of generations of species and a multitude of human cultures. I had the same sensation I get when I look into a night sky at the stars and realize just how far away they are. In the presence of these trees, I felt like a mere blink in time and space. And I was humbled.

If the coast redwood's lifespan challenges the perspective of the decades I have on earth, imagining the lifespan of a stone, measured in millions of years, has a similar effect on me. As remarkable and inspiring as the living, natural world is to me in all her abundance, rocks still enthrall me. Like most children, I loved collecting stones, putting them in my pockets, then lining them along a windowsill. Happily, my parents facilitated this early childhood fascination and took us on fossil-hunting expeditions. I hungered to find crystals and precious stones, and I coveted many a rock at retail stores and venues that sold such items.

I was thrilled to discover that my own children gathered stones in their pockets, and Santa even delivered a rock polisher to our eldest daughter, Elena, one Christmas. Now, I love to watch my granddaughter sitting happily in the middle of a driveway of pebbles, sifting them through her fingers.

I am flooded with many memories of rocks and stones as

I write—watching Harvey skip beautifully colored flat granite stones gathered from the shore of a glacial lake, buying a turquoise-colored rock for my daughter just because it was pretty, the brain-shaped rock covered in fossilized coral that my father found and that still lives at my parents' house, and gathering and saving small pebbles from my travels.

Then there are my memories of the solid stone walls of the Grand Canyon in all its multi-hued splendor, and the fantastical formations at Bryce Canyon and Arches National Park. Or the sheer cliffs of distant shores in England and Italy, and nearer ones in Yosemite. Or incredibly high pinnacles of majestic mountains of stone in Spain, Switzerland, and Colorado.

When I meditate, I like to place myself, in my mind's eye, on a sunny boulder in the middle of a stream situated in a deep forest. The solidness of the rock grounds me as the melody of the waters dance, and a breeze gently lifts the hairs on my arms. With all my senses engaged, I can just be.

As ephemeral as life is in all its varieties, the rocks endure. Yes, weathering does eventually erode them, but stone will still outlast the longest-living organism. The decay and rebirth of a plant into a new generation or the transformation of caterpillar into butterfly is a miracle, but so too is the persistence of mineral, even as it wears to sand.

It gives me comfort to know that my brief life is but a moment in the life of a stone. It places my problems and frustrations into a perspective that lessens their hold over me. Yes, what I do matters, but the rocks tell me that my concerns are small. Because my time on earth is relatively short, what I do and say really does matter if I want to make a difference and live a life of abundance, joy, and love.

Imagine all that the stones and redwoods have seen and heard, bearing silent witness to life's transitory passages. It's all a matter of perspective.

My first real aha moment with thinking about perspective

was when I was in science class in elementary school. We were shown a film where the opening shot was of a boy and his grandfather fishing from a small boat on a lake. The camera then slowly moved closer, focusing on the boy, then his face, his eye, then the interior of his eye, zooming closer to show the microscopic structure of the retina at a cellular level. Closer still into the makeup of one cell, the nucleus, then the tightly wound DNA, the compounds that compose that DNA, then an individual atom of carbon, and finally an electron whirling around the nucleus of the atom. The camera then slowly retreated back to the shot of the boy and his grandfather, but it continued to move ever farther back to show the lake, then the surrounding forest, and farther and farther away until we saw Earth as a whole, and still farther to include our galaxy and beyond.

I think this film moved me, even as a child, on many levels. I had always been fascinated with science, and here it all was, in a fifteen-minute film. The scope and breadth of the natural world is staggering, and so is the human capacity to understand it. It also raised the question of the limits of our knowledge—what is beyond our understanding on a micro and a macro scale?

This little film, and concepts like it, filled me with wonder. Yes, wonder at the marvelous natural world we live in, and especially awe of its complexity, intricacy, and vastness. If the words were available to me at the time, I would have said that *this* is why I believe there is a God.

But if we are each individuals, living our individual lives separate from each other, in a hermetically sealed bubble of natural wonder, would that be enough of an experience to fully know and understand the Divine? No. It is with each other—in one-on-one interactions, in our families, in our faith communities, in our neighborhoods, and in the larger human community—that we develop an even deeper understanding of the Divine.

There is a teaching from Dorotheus of Gaza, a Desert Father, from about 540 CE that has long held deep meaning for me. He asks us to imagine a wheel, with the Divine at the center hub and all of humankind spread out on the circumference, or rim. As we move closer to the Divine, down our particular spoke of this wheel, we necessarily move closer to each other. Too, if we move toward one another, we will move toward the Divine. What a beautiful interplay. This interaction reminds me of Jesus's teaching that the greatest commandments are to love God and to love each other. Conversely, if we pull away from the center hub, the Divine, we also move away from a deeper understanding of, and connection with, others. And if we isolate ourselves from humanity, we are further from the Divine.

I certainly felt this dynamic during the years of Harvey's illness. I wouldn't have been able to name it as *Divine* at the time. It actually felt like any form of Divine presence was very far from us in this bleakness. But the comfort and support of those who cared for us were reminders that the Divine uses human hands and feet to do the work. It is from the distance of time that I can fully appreciate this truth. It's kind of like that film. When I zoom in on the particulars of all that others did for us, I am amazed. And when I pull back and take a look through a much larger lens, I see the Divine all over the place.

I have one more story on perspective, and it relates a lesson that I learned from a former patient of mine, Mrs. Johnson. Several years ago, she experienced an acute neurologic emergency. Fortunately, she was rushed to the emergency room in time and had surgery that halted progression of the emergency. Unfortunately, she was left with some cognitive impairment. Always a high achiever at work, a manager with several employees answering to her, she had been able to juggle many tasks, make quick decisions, and carry a large workload. After struggling for months after her neurosurgery, Mrs. Johnson asked for accommodations at her job. She was given fewer responsibilities, and the quota for the amount of work she was asked to produce was reduced. She finally retired nine months later, unable and unwilling to manage the stress and mental challenge of even these reduced job responsibilities.

As her family physician, I was helping Mrs. Johnson navigate her new life. She told me that once she retired, her days were long and restful. She found herself not doing much of anything at times, and at other times, she would be productive. She wasn't anxious or depressed about the situation, and, in fact, was enjoying this new pace her life was taking.

However, whenever her husband came home from work, he would always ask her, "So, what did you do today?" *This* is what was stressful for her. Mrs. Johnson felt put on the spot, trying to defend how she had spent her day while he had been working. Eventually, she responded to this daily question by turning the tables and saying, "Honey, I'd rather you just ask me how my day was instead."

Light bulbs flashed in my head when she told me this story. How many times had I dreaded that same question, and asked it myself?

When Harvey and I practiced medicine together, we alternated days at the office seeing patients with days at home parenting our two daughters. When the one of us with the full day at the clinic would come home, we would greet each other with "So, what did you do today?" Harvey would have no trouble answering this question. He would give a blow-by-blow account of his day, usually entailing yard work, playing with the kids, and taking walks with them and the dog. I, on the other hand, dreaded that question. "Nothing much" wouldn't cut it. "Shopping" sounded too frivolous. "Meeting a friend and her kids for lunch" sounded too self-centered. I would rehearse my answer before he came home, racking my brain for something productive to report, grateful when I could report just washing a load of laundry.

That question—"What did you do today?"—picked up a whole new set of baggage when Harvey was diagnosed with Alzheimer's disease and forced to retire. I continued to ask him that question every day when I got home from the office. Only, he could not always remember what he had done. He would try. There was the usual "walked the dog" and "picked up the carpool," things he would do every day, but sometimes there was nothing else that he could report. I had no way of knowing how he spent his day if he could not remember enough of it to tell me. When I finally realized that asking that question was causing Harvey more stress about his fading memory, I felt guilty, and just quit asking.

This is when Mrs. Johnson told me her story. I began to ask Harvey "How was your day today?" when I got home from the office, and he would respond in all sorts of ways. Sometimes he said, "Great! I got a lot done." Sometimes he said, "It was OK." Sometimes he gave me a complete description of his day. But the ball was now in his court. The pressure I was placing on him to remember what he had done during the day was replaced by a more genuine desire for me to understand how he was feeling about the day. I began to use this new version of the question with my daughters after school, and with my elderly parents.

Patients taught me things all the time. Such a simple one, but this lesson of reframing a basic question, looking at it from a different perspective, was one of the best.

Sometimes reframing an entire situation, not just a simple question, looking at a perceived problem with new eyes, can carry you through a challenging time. Focusing in on the details of a difficult situation can blur you to the bigger picture.

For example, a person who is living with dementia may be fighting against taking a shower, not to be ornery, but because the shower is an unknown, unseen force that beats down on them. Stepping back and seeing the shower from their perspective helps your understanding and may limit your frustration.

Try seeing the people around you as their whole selves, seeing the forest of their lives as well as their trees. If you only focus on what you are confronted with in the moment, your limited perspective may hinder your ability to offer the best care or support. You are more than the person who awoke this morning. You have lived a life, traveled many roads, accumulating multiple insights on this life. So, too, has every other person you encounter.

Gain a new perspective on grief and loss; it will not last forever. It's just a period of time in your life. It will be in your past at some point. When you look back on this time of your life, you just might see more beauty than you can possibly imagine when you are in the thick of it. Not that you should minimize your grief or struggles, because naming and honoring a particular time of hardship is important. But maybe by shifting your focus to the bigger picture of your life, realizing the whole of it is more than this one point in time, some of your pain can lessen.

And stepping back even further to view a longer perspective can give you a moment to pause and breathe a prayer of gratitude for the life you have.

CHAPTER 3

Walking with Community

Once, while staying at a dear friend's home on Lake Martin in central Alabama, I hiked a very challenging and narrow, twisting trail along the shores of this lake. All I could do was keep my eyes down and follow the path.

While on that hike, a memory emerged of an experience I had of walking a labyrinth. I think that the trail shook this memory from me because it was so like a maze with its twists and turns, and I had no clear idea of where I was going. I was just following the path wherever it led me.

Unlike a maze, a labyrinth has only one path from the outer edge, moving you forward, and leading you to its center. After reaching the center of the labyrinth, you then make your way back out following the same path that you took into it, but in reverse. It can be a spiritual and transformative practice, a type of walking meditation that might act as a metaphor for journeying to the center of yourself, then carrying that spark of divinity out into the world. There are no dead ends or tricks. You cannot lose your way—it's a tool that helps you find your way.

About two months prior to Harvey's official diagnosis, I participated in a labyrinth event sponsored by Veriditas, an organization that facilitates labyrinth experiences. I had walked several labyrinths in the past—some guided, some alone—and I was excited to see what this particular labyrinth walk had to teach me. However, my excitement turned to dread when the facilitator asked us to carry this question into the labyrinth: "What in you needs healing?"

All the fear, sadness, anxiety, and anger I was bottling inside, because I knew what his diagnosis was going to be, washed over me. As I walked the labyrinth, to quiet my mind from the swirling thoughts and emotions, I began to repeat to myself, "I am walking this path, and I don't know where it leads. I will walk in trust."

Almost immediately, I realized that the labyrinth's path was a metaphor for my life's path, and my mantra turned into "I don't *want* to be on this path. I want off this path. I want to leave." I could have stepped out of the labyrinth and run away, but I stayed, stopped in my tracks, and sobbed. It *was* my path. I was going to have to walk it.

One of the profound aspects of walking a labyrinth is walking it in community. Because it is laid out on the ground, one can see the entire pathway as a whole, and all the participants who are walking in the different quadrants of it. From the outside, it looks like a beautiful dance. From the inside, each participant is a part of the dance of the whole community. And a community was there that day to support me, even if they knew nothing of my inner turmoil.

After a few more episodes of tears, I was able to gather myself and be reminded that although Harvey and I were on our own unique paths, our friends and family members would walk alongside us, just as the fellow seekers on the labyrinth were walking alongside me. We wouldn't be alone on this journey.

Once in the center, I paused and took several deep breaths, trying to connect with my center—my authentic self, the godspark within, the inner Divine. I picked up a smooth white stone with gray striations from a collection of rocks that had been placed there. Carrying the stone out of the labyrinth, I carried myself out into the world. After I completed my walk, I watched as others continued their individual journeys. I beheld the whole of the labyrinth as a symbol for a single life among community. We each walk our own path, but we are accompanied by others, and the whole of the journey is what makes us who we are. And the whole is beautiful in its complexity and balance.

Back to that twisting trail along the shore of Lake Martin. At one point, the path rose to a crest, and I was struck by the sight of bright orange splashed on several rock surfaces. It looked as if the rocks were rusting in patches or like someone had carelessly spilled paint on the stones. When I looked more closely, I saw that the splotches of color were, in fact, lichens.

Lichens are ancient, long-lived, but easily overlooked organisms that take on many forms and colors. They grow on a variety of substrates, from tree trunks to rock faces. You've likely seen lichens all your life but never paid much attention to them. And yet they are fascinating and can teach us about interconnectedness and community.

Lichens are not plants. They don't have leaves or roots, and they can't transport nutrients through the complex system developed by plants. They are actually a combination of an alga and a fungus. Rarely do the individual components exist alone. They are mutually dependent on, and beneficial to, each other.

The algae produce sugars through photosynthesis, which provides nourishment for themselves and the fungal elements. In fact, over 50 percent of the sugars produced by the algae are taken by the fungus. The fungus provides physical protection to the fragile algae and captures water and minerals for them both. In biology, this is called *symbiosis*. It's not a parasitic relationship because they both thrive in the company of the other.

Scientists have a hard time growing lichens in the laboratory. The separate components grow if conditions are excellent for each, but they won't come together to form the lichen. Interestingly, only when conditions are harsh and extreme do the algae and fungus merge to create a lichen, helping each other survive in a mutually beneficial relationship.

Digging deeper, the structure of lichens is intriguing. Although lichens take many physical forms, the predominant structure is as follows: The surface is usually made up of hyphae, fungal threads that are tightly bound together to form a thin but protective roof for the delicate algae. Beneath that, the fungal hyphae form a looser web, holding the algae between their threads. Below that, there is an even looser tangle of fungal hyphae that traps and holds water. The bottom-most layer is made up of fungal attachments to the substrate. Here, using enzymes, the fungus can break down the rock or bark, releasing the minerals within and then distributing them among the fungal and algae elements. When it rains, water penetrates the outer coat, turning the surface transparent. Now the algae can begin to photosynthesize, and the lichen's surface visually turns green.

Isn't this the way community and partnership should work? Each component doing its part for the whole, dependent on the gifts and talents each member brings. Community functions best when we are dependent on each other. We are not made to go it alone. Especially when conditions are difficult, we need to come together to nourish and support each other. In Christian teaching, Paul uses the analogy of the human body, all its parts working together to form a highly functioning whole. Together, the whole is greater than the sum of the parts.

As caregivers to children, aging parents, or ailing friends and family, and, actually, as human beings in the world, we cannot "do life" all by ourselves. We may try, but eventually, we will need to ask for help or at least accept the help that is offered. The parent or caregiver's job is to try to make sure that their loved ones are safe and content. This, and other aspects of running a household, can become overwhelming, and outsourcing may become necessary. Turning to our friends, family, and other members of our community provides us with support and nourishment so that we can embody the role of primary caregiver in the healthiest way possible.

STRONGER TOGETHER

Early in Harvey's time with Alzheimer's disease, I often felt the need to explain his odd words and behaviors because I was embarrassed by them. This was almost always with strangers—the young mother of a toddler who he was trying to interact with, the barista who was only trying to be friendly, but who he blatantly ignored. I didn't feel the need so strongly to explain what was happening when we were among friends and close family. They knew. They accepted. They supported. Beyond the tangible ways they offered support, there was also an invisible support, not tied to deeds or words. I felt such a support when walking the labyrinth with community, and when I sat in the congregation of my church.

This kind of invisible support is something I frequently ruminated on while hiking in nature, surrounded by the forest, an ecosystem that is really a community made up of all the plant life—from tiny mushrooms to large mother trees—and all the animal life supported there. The larger trees' canopies provide shade and shelter for the smaller plants and animals below. Sunlight provides energy for the trees and other plants, and that energy is converted into foodstuffs for the animals. In turn, animal waste, and their eventual decay, provides nutrients to the plants.

The magic really happens in the ground below, invisible to human eyes. There's a whole hidden world below the surface of the earth that supports and nourishes life both in the soil and above it. Think roots, earthworms, certain insects, and the remarkable interconnectedness of trees and fungi.

Mushrooms are the outward and visible signs of the unseen subterranean world of fungi. They are the fruiting bodies, the part of the fungus that is responsible for reproduction. The fine filamentous fungal hyphae are underground, spreading sometime miles-wide in the earth, forming a vast interlaced network. Minute strands of fungal hyphae create a web in the soil that connects trees and other plants with each other.

Using the underground "wood wide web" of fungal hyphae, trees communicate with and support each other. We only see the mushroom, but that structure is just a tip of the iceberg for fungi. Using this system, trees will divert nourishment from thriving specimens to ones that are floundering, forgoing their own abundance for the needs of their failing neighbors. Trees can also warn each other of imminent danger, such as pests, through these fungal hyphae as well as through chemicals released by leaves into the atmosphere, which are then carried by the wind.

This silent, invisible support is what I experienced during the years of Harvey's illness and afterward. Even without having to explain what was happening at home, I felt understood by those closest to me, as well as by the greater community of which we were a part. My family and I sheltered in the shade of our community. The life-giving energy of those around us gave each of us the courage to take the next best step. We were not asked to contribute but were fed and nourished. We were held and supported by all the deep roots that intertwined with ours. We did not fall when the storms of Harvey's disease wreaked havoc in our lives.

On my trip to Northern California with friends, this aspect of silent community support became even more apparent. Though I experienced community with these friends, it was the forest community of coastal redwoods that strengthened the conviction that it is only with community that we can make our way. Because the coast redwoods are so enormous, one would think that they reproduce using massive cones. However, their cones are only the size of an olive, and each tree produces fifty to sixty tiny seeds in the autumn. The chances that one of these seeds will land in soil with perfect conditions and germinate is minuscule.

I learned about another way these trees reproduce when I visited Muir Woods National Monument—family circles. As an avid reader of informational signage when in a new locale, I learned that when a coast redwood dies or is cut down, new shoots arise around its periphery, out of the fallen tree's existing roots. The shoots then grow independently, drawing water and nutrients from the original tree's roots that are already established. Because the canopy is now gone, and the sky has been opened, sunlight is available for the new growth. Eventually, a circle of mature redwoods forms around the place where the first tree, the mother tree, stood.

I saw these circles throughout the park, usually surrounding a large redwood that had succumbed to fire, its remaining trunk hollowed and blackened. In a ring around their fallen mother, these genetic clones formed a tight circle, each a giant in its own right, reaching a height of over two hundred feet in some rings.

These circles of sisters are beautiful pictures of community. A deceased elder of a community, like the original tree, still has power by virtue of the deep metaphorical roots they previously sank. The root system is their wealth of wisdom and experience, and it sustains younger members of the community as they bring forth new growth while carrying the elder's innate intelligence forward.

A circle is eternal, not linear. Wisdom is not always passed down from one member to another in a linear progression. Rather, it can be an outward expansion, like spreading ripples in water. One life has an effect on those closest to them, then the legacy of their life experiences expands ever wider. Imagine a human community as a forest of these circles.

Most deciduous tree root systems are as deep as the tree is tall. For the coast redwood, even though they can stand over three hundred feet, their roots are only about twelve feet deep. These massive giants remain upright when gale-force winds blow because their roots are intertwined with their neighbors'. An individual tree relies on the strength of community to keep standing. This is how community is supposed to function. Only by supporting one another can one person withstand the blows life sends.

Common garden-variety ants taught me another lesson in community one day while I was sitting on my front patio, journaling. I caught some slight movement out of the corner of my eye, and turning my head, I saw what looked like a bit of dead leaf moving slowly across the ground, floating just above the surface. Looking more closely, I could see that ants seemed to be transporting this bit of leaf. Then I got on my hands and knees for an even closer look. Yes, about twelve ants were moving a tiny piece of a dead leaf across my patio, and there were other lone ants dashing about in front and behind the team. I watched as the ants and their leaf made their way to the edge of the patio.

At that edge is an electric cord. How were the ants going to maneuver their treasure over this obstacle? I watched as they first tried going over it directly, but they couldn't seem to get traction on the slick black cylindrical cord. They traveled down the length of cord a bit and tried to go under it, but that didn't work either. At a spot a little farther down, there seemed to be a rise in the patio. The ants had their opportunity, and as a team, they got their prize over the cord.

I was intrigued. Where were they going? What were they going to do with this bit of dead leaf? I didn't see any ant mounds looming, so I continued to study them as they made their way over and under the leaf litter between the clumps of miniature monkey grass that make up my lawn. Eventually I lost them. I never figured out where they took their treasure.

I knew that ants are extremely strong for their size, but I had never heard of them cooperating to transport an unwieldy piece of leaf on the level that I witnessed on my patio. With some research, I found out that, sure enough, ants will work together to move an object that they want. Ants don't have hands and fingers, so they grab the object with their mouths and pull in the direction they want to go. The seemingly random ants who are not carrying the object are actually sniffing the air for the location of the final destination. One of these scout ants then grasps the object and pulls harder than the rest of the ants, guiding the team to more effectively move the object toward the goal.

What a powerful metaphor for providing care, or even just for living. When there is a substantial goal that needs to be achieved, we need a team to help us with the heavy lifting. We can't do it alone. And when we are working hard, heads down, moving forward, we may lose sight of that goal. We need scouts to look at the situation with new eyes and a fresh take, then be strong enough to guide us, and our team, toward the goal.

※※※

The absolute hardest physical challenge of my life has been climbing Mount Kilimanjaro, and that trip exemplifies the metaphor of a supportive organism, complete with scouts and leaders and a team. Our group could not have reached the summit without all of us working together.

Our group of eight—two leaders in their early thirties, one woman in her fifties, and five of us in our sixties—were a tight-knight group, focused as we were on the goal. All of us knew at least two others beforehand, but we had not all coalesced as a community until we met and gelled over our shared goal and love of adventure. No one person dominated. We all listened to our leaders and guides. There was no dissent among the ranks. As the week progressed, the glue that held us together became ever stronger as we encouraged and congratulated each other with each new day. When one person in our group became too ill to continue, it affected us all. We supported her completely in her decision to head back down the mountain. We felt the loss as a group, but we rallied again in our common goal.

What we absolutely could not have done without was the support of our army of porters and guides. In the first communication we received with information about the trip, we learned that we would be shepherded by over forty local men and women. I was astounded! Why in the world would we need forty people, a ratio of five to one, to help our small group of Americans up the mountain?

That army included four official guides, two cooks, two waiters, two dishwashers, two men responsible for procuring and filtering our daily water supply, two people who set up and took down all the tents, two men who cleaned and maintained our latrines, and a cook for the porters. There was also one porter designated to carry each group member's duffel bag. That's a total of twenty-three. The remainder carried the rest of the camp's equipment.

Each day after our morning meal, the eight of us donned

our small daypacks and set off with the guides. The remaining crew of porters then dismantled all the tents and equipment, packing up the kitchen and latrines, as well as their own personal gear. Then they loaded these burdens onto their heads or necks, as well as their own backpacks, and went up the trail, swiftly passing our group. Each porter, whether they were from our team or another, greeted us with a cheerful "Jambo!" ("Hello!") as they climbed past us to the next campsite. When we finally arrived at each day's camp, the porters had already completely set it up for us.

This whole operation was a wonder. Our group of eight was exquisitely well taken care of so that we could use our resources only for the trek itself. So little was required of us beyond just getting from one camp to the next.

In community, there is reciprocity and mutual caring for each member, and our group of eight did feel like community. But the army of porters was a community of its own. Even though it was their job, the cheerfulness, kindness, and care exhibited by the porters toward our group were genuine. The whole of our experience on the mountain was more like a nurturing. It was as if we were children being looked after and encouraged by loving parents.

There are times in our lives when we do need looking after, when all our internal resources are being used just to put one foot in front of the other, maintaining our physical, mental, or spiritual equilibrium. We rely on community when we cannot accomplish life's tasks alone.

GRATITUDE IN COMMUNITY

Ash Wednesday is the somber first day of Lent, the Christian season leading up to Easter, specifically the forty days, not including Sundays, that precede Easter. Traditionally, it has been seen as a time for personal reflection, fasting, and prayer. The practice of giving something up for Lent comes from the centuries-old Christian Lenten observance of abstaining from meat, wine, oil, and dairy products.

Other than fasting, some choose to give up luxuries such as alcohol, social media, animal products, or watching television. I have occasionally chosen to give up something for Lent, usually a food item to which I felt addicted. I noticed that when I craved potato chips or a chocolate bar, it gave me a chance to reflect on my unhealthy desire and to be reminded that the true source of spiritual sustenance is not found in what I put in my mouth. Others choose to add a positive habit instead—prayer, reading holy texts, exercising, or volunteering.

A few years ago, my friend Becky chose to take on a positive discipline for Lent. Becky's mother, Carolyn, had dementia, and her care was weighing heavily on Becky, as it does for all caregivers at some point. The burden of all Becky's responsibilities was adding up, and it also felt like Carolyn was no longer the same woman Becky had known all her life. Caring for her mother was clouding her feelings of love.

As a Lenten practice, Becky decided to create a gratitude journal. Instead of the usual practice of writing about all the people and things that one is thankful for, though, Becky began to write memories of her mother, one thought per day. It became a journal of thanks for all the ways Carolyn had made an impact on Becky and on the world. This practice transformed the relationship between Becky and her mother. She was able to remember Carolyn as the person she had always been before the diagnosis, and the burden of caregiving morphed into a deeper commitment to the woman who had nurtured and cared for her as a child and beyond. Throughout daily challenges, this practice helped Becky remember that she loved her mother but hated the disease. Gratitude will change a person.

Scientific studies have shown that gratitude can improve

your mental health. You can create a long-lasting effect by shifting your focus toward thankfulness, and away from negative or toxic thoughts. This occurs in healthy individuals as well as in people experiencing depression or anxiety. Even if your gratitude is written only for yourself and not shared, the benefits persist for a significant amount of time.

Writing my memoir was a form of gratitude as I named each person in my community who walked alongside Harvey, our daughters, and me for the duration of, and after, his time with dementia. I still tear up thinking about the countless, selfless ways our community showed up for us. I am also grateful for the community of professionals and their services as they supported us. I am grateful for the people I have met who are on their own journey with this disease, or other hardships, and their willingness to share their stories and singular perspectives.

I am a strong person, born that way, raised that way, but I cannot do life, especially the hard parts, alone. It takes community, a village, to support its members through all of life's transitions and challenges. Even after learning this lesson many times, I still forget to ask for help when I should. Chagrin washes over me when a friend suggests a way they could help—chagrin that I hadn't thought to ask, and chagrin that I still am uncomfortable asking for and receiving help, even after all that has passed.

Back in the redwoods, I ended my trip by standing in the center of one of the family circles, contemplating that huge ring of trees descended from one. I offered a prayer of gratitude for all the people in my life, those still present, and those who are now gone, who have gifted me with their strength and their wisdom. I continue to draw on that wealth as I grow in the light they left behind.

And as I plan for my future now, I realize I will necessarily need more support as I age, and that sometimes fills me with dread. I don't want to put my family and friends in a position of having to help me. I'd rather take care of it myself. But that's not the way community works. It's reciprocal. I served my community of patients, then community supported me through Harvey's disease, and now I am caring for a wider community through my writing and speaking. My turn to rely on community again will come. As we journey through life, we will need guides and support, visible and invisible, just as we are guides and support to others, and that should fill us with gratitude.

PART TWO

Moving Onward

ALZHEIMER'S BEAUTIFUL SCARS

The scars on the tree are beautiful
Built up over time, they heal
And strengthen the tree.
Now there's a hole
Where it once was whole
And through it,
I can see the forest
That once was blocked from view.

The scars in his brain are not beautiful
The holes in his memory
Have replaced the whole
Of who he was.

He can no longer plan or reminisce
He can only live in the present,
Dragging me back to the now.
Is this a gift?

But look.
Through the holes in his brain
I can see the boy.

Stripped of the ego the man built
As armor against the world,
The boy shines through.

I see the boy that he was,
Fascinated by the wonders of
Balloons and bubbles.
Playing and dancing and singing together,
In ways we never did when he was whole.

I never knew him as a boy,
But maybe now I do.
In this present moment,
His scar is beautiful.

CHAPTER 4

Trails and Trials

We live in a world of water, and on my second day of hiking in Switzerland, that fact was evidenced by how I and five other middle-aged female alpine trekkers spent most of that day in the rain.

The day started with a propitious rainbow at sunrise, the mountaintops glowing a brilliant tangerine. We knew this would be the hardest and longest hike of our trip, lasting fifteen miles and having about a four-thousand-foot elevation gain. After filling our backpack bladders with cool, fresh water from the town's trough and checking the forecast, we set out in our rain gear. We were quickly met with fog and mist—the kind of mist that lightly kissed our faces. It turned into a harder rain as we entered a deep forest of evergreens and moss, where Hansel and Gretel surely wandered. The forest gave cover for the precipitation, but when we emerged onto a meadow, the wind began blowing, and the rain pelted our faces with tiny arrows. As it picked up, we kept our heads down and trudged on. Because we were in this together, though, our spirits remained high. The rain actually made the trek more pleasant at times, washing away our sweat. We were united as a group as conversation flowed, and we took on the elements together.

At a section of the trail that was to lead us around the edge of a lake, there were barriers and warnings not to pass. Our leaders looked at their maps and decided on an alternative route, one that followed a road up the mountain to Grimsel Pass, our destination. Walking single file in the drainage ditch of this narrow two-lane road, we made our way through a steady rain, now somehow refreshing and annoying at the same time.

The rain continued as we approached the last section of the trail, a series of steep hairpin turns through heavy fog. We were wet, cold, and exhausted when distant thunder began rolling around the mountains. The trail itself was flowing with water as the falling rain made its way over the rocky path. We stopped often to hydrate and catch our breaths, our exhalations like small clouds. The friendly banter dissipated. The only spoken words now came from our leaders, offering encouragement.

By the end of the day's trek, our perspiration mingled with the rain, our feet were soaked, and our limbs were liquid with fatigue. At Grimsel Pass, we revived ourselves with rounds of hot chocolate and congratulations.

That day was a day of water, in many forms: water stored as cloud and fog, rain as drizzle and downpour, rivers and streams and waterfalls and lakes, water ingested, sweat on our bodies, rivulets on the trail. We were one with the water for most of the day. Our human bodies are made up of mostly water, but on this day, our bodies were also part of the larger world of water—immersed, enveloped, and buoyed by it. What seemed like an obstacle to our trek became a lesson in taking one step at a time, facing whatever presented itself and making peace with it.

ONE STEP AT A TIME

While hiking, I have also encountered water as another kind of obstacle—in the form of streams or rivers. There is usually a way to cross, and I've only ever turned back once when faced with a difficult stream. In that case, I could make out a ladder on the opposite shore that was there to assist in climbing the far bank, but it was partly submerged. Photos on my hiking app showed a much lower water level relative to the ladder, and it did state that you might have to wade through the creek to reach the ladder on the other side. This looked like more than wading, so I decided against it. I met two park rangers farther down my alternate trail, and they said that the water was probably waist high where I was considering crossing. I had chosen correctly.

We came across a number of bridges while on the group hiking trek in the Alps—some ordinary, some extraordinary. There were several wooden plank bridges crossing small streams, and a few longer ones with handrails, just like the ones I have used at home. These simple bridges allowed me to cross the water without getting my feet wet.

My favorite bridges in the Alps were constructed from stone that had been quarried from the surrounding area. These sported a gentle arch, some with a keystone set at the apex of the curve. The stones had weathered with a patina of lichens and moss. I have no idea how old they were, but they looked as if they could have come from a fairy tale, perhaps the one about the three billy goats and the troll who dared them to cross.

The most spectacular bridge we encountered in Switzerland

was a long suspension bridge tethered on either side of a deep gorge. With the wind whipping through the canyon, those of us who dared gripped tightly to the two strong cables with each hand. The first few wooden slats were steep, so cross bars had been added for better traction. It bounced a bit, of course, and swayed in the wind, and even though it felt very secure, there was absolutely a measure of fear in crossing it.

Bridges make for great metaphors for some of life's passages. Some crossings in our lives are simple and require little to provide a means to get from here to there. Maybe a milestone such as orthodontia, a first pair of glasses, or a decision to start a new friendship could be seen this way. You can't correct an unhealthy bite or poor vision without the aid. You can't have a friendship without first reaching out.

Graduation from school may be a simple bridge for some, but it might need to be longer and stronger for others. A hard-won promotion, a birth, a marriage, a divorce, a cure for a simple illness—these most likely come with a quite sturdy bridge, with handrails and good traction—there are clear steps to take that have been tested by others, and you simply follow the prescribed path.

Other obstacles in life, great chasms of hardship, will need to be crossed by the more tenuous suspension bridge. Or at least, that's how it feels. How do you get to the other side of this gaping canyon of illness, suffering, or grief? By taking one step at a time, watching your feet and holding your breath while the wind whistles around you and you feel the depth of the fall if you slip. By holding on tightly to the guylines placed by those who went first. By knowing that others have crossed this bridge before. By trusting that the bridge will hold and taking tentative steps at first until you are surer of your footing.

If a bridge isn't available, sometimes stepping stones provide another way to get to the other side of a stream while hiking. One of my favorite sets of stepping stones crosses a stream on a city walking path that regularly floods. The city also built a high, sturdy bridge across the creek, but I still prefer the concrete stepping stones. They are placed exactly to fit my stride, and I can maintain my walking pace and cross the stream without breaking my rhythm. It's almost as if I am walking on the surface of the water.

When I hike, I enjoy crossing small creeks using stepping stones, ones either deliberately placed, or just naturally occurring. First, I scan the layout and decide my initial step. I might test out the first stone's stability by rocking my foot on its surface before stepping onto it. If I know my next step, I might just go ahead and take it, and the next, lightly hopping across the stream. Sometimes, however, the best path isn't always clear, and I have to judge each step going forward. Or change plans if the original one turns out to have too far of a stretch or a jump. It can be tricky. I've even created my own stepping stone path by placing rocks where I needed them to be. Balance, foot-eye coordination, and leg strength all play into the equation. At times, I have had to hike along the bank of a creek for some distance in order to find a suitable crossing.

Always on the lookout for metaphors, I see one in stepping stones, illustrating how to navigate a difficult situation. If you break down a difficult task into the smaller steps that need to be taken, the wide expanse ahead doesn't seem as daunting. When I looked at the long game of my medical education, I was easily overwhelmed and discouraged, but when I took it one course at a time, one year at a time, it was more manageable to contemplate. When Harvey was diagnosed with Alzheimer's disease, it felt catastrophic to look too far into the future. One step at a time, one day at a time, was far easier. Similarly, when I look ahead to a life without Harvey, I can be overcome with sadness. Yet, somehow, when I wake up each morning and plan my day's activities, the sadness gives way to anticipation.

Stepping stones provide us with a way to get from here to

there, one step at a time. We may falter as we decide which next step to take, balancing precariously on the last stone. We might need to lay down a stone we have been carrying in order for it to be used as a stepping stone. We might accidentally step into the stream and get wet, but we have learned something in the process. Once on the opposite bank, we can look back and see how far we have come and the steps that led us to safety.

Hiking a trail isn't always smooth going. Oh, how many times I have tripped over a rock or a root! Sometimes it's because I didn't pick up my foot high enough. At other times, especially if the rock was hidden beneath leaves or pine straw, I would trip over it. The obscured rock would cause me to stumble along the trail until I regained my balance. Or fell. I have fallen due to turning an ankle on a rock that I didn't see because I was looking out at the trail ahead instead of at the path at my feet. And I took a really bad tumble once when hiking at a fast clip, catching the toe of my boot on a root. These were each a stumbling block along the trail.

But can stumbling blocks become stepping stones—taking you to a new understanding? Often, we don't view those stumbling blocks as stepping stones until they cause us to trip up and force a change in direction. Looking back with a new perspective, we can view those stumbling blocks as stepping stones.

When I practiced medicine, certain patients were sometimes stumbling blocks to my schedule. When someone spent an inordinate amount of time describing their concerns or the story that led up to their current situation, I would scream internally, *Just get to the point already!* Eventually I learned to accept their desire to tell their story, in the way they needed, to a concerned listener. Such patients became stepping stones to greater patience and better skill at directing the flow of the encounter.

I can create my own stumbling blocks in my mind, too,

making mountains out of molehills. When I view a difficult situation as an obstacle, I might falter, stop in my tracks, make halting attempts, and sometimes even turn back. I rarely view the blocks as stepping stones until the difficulty has passed and I can reflect on what lessons I have learned.

When caring for Harvey, I frequently stumbled with situations that I didn't see coming. I thought I was prepared, as a physician, to handle all the situations that might arise. I knew he had a medical condition, and that changes to his behavior were occurring because of the condition. But whenever I mis-stepped, it was usually because I didn't see it coming. I reacted to the situation as if it were an obstacle and not a stepping stone to a broader understanding of what was happening to him.

The best example I can think of is when Harvey wandered from home while I was away. There was no warning that this might be something he would do, but of course, there is always the first time a behavior occurs. His wandering became one of the stepping stones that led me to hire in-home care and enroll him in respite care.

My stumbling blocks these days are doubt, indecision, insecurity, and silence about the next paths I should take in my life. I've been grappling with "what's next" for a long time now, and when I trip over these thoughts, I get nowhere. But when I view the intrusive thoughts as stepping stones, the way becomes clearer.

Thoughts of self-doubt lead to affirmation when I can see my past successes as stepping stones. For example, when deciding whether or not I had anything to say in a second book, I could look to the first and remind myself that it did indeed have the outcome I had hoped for—people who read it were encouraged and uplifted by our story.

Indecision becomes an opportunity to see in many directions. There may be many paths forward, and having plenty of them to choose from is a blessing. I am not beholden to one way forward. Trying to decide where to travel and venture to next, I can become overwhelmed with choices, but the research leads me to appreciate all that there is to see in the world.

Insecurity becomes self-confidence as I look back over all that I have overcome. I remind myself that I am a strong, independent woman. If I could handle all the responsibilities of the clinic and the household, I can surely tackle a tree that falls and damages my roof, for example.

Silence from the Universe becomes a lesson in patience.

Sometimes there aren't stepping stones, or even a clear path to follow. I always try to be prepared before hiking—especially if I'm going alone. The hiking app I use helps me find trails wherever I'm visiting. I review the area's available trails for length and difficulty, reading the comments, too, to see if I need my hiking poles and to gain any bit of wisdom from previous hikers. But there is no way to be completely certain about the trail ahead.

I found a promising trail off the popular Devil's Courthouse stop on the Blue Ridge Parkway in North Carolina. I first hiked the steep, paved incline to the views at the courthouse, then I took off down the trail I was planning to hike. When I came to the loop portion, I veered right, as the hiking app showed. But the trail petered out. Or I couldn't find it. Or I was just lost. This was a deep, dark evergreen forest, my favorite kind of forest. Trails through these kinds of woods are usually carpeted with pine needles, creating a soft, cushiony path. Off the trail, the forest floor itself was especially dense with needles and layers of fallen, decaying trees. I was thrashing around, holding my phone like a compass, trying to match my location to the trail, and worried that I would step in a hole in this deep forest floor or trip on something I couldn't see. I wasn't worried about wild animals; I was making too much noise crunching around.

I finally gave up and made my way back to the start of the loop and decided to go in the opposite direction. This was an obvious, well-marked trail. I came to the point where the loop returned, but again, nothing but dense, spongy underbrush. Yes, I stomped around again, looking for this portion of the trail, but to no avail. I gave up again and turned around, retracing my steps on the serviceable trail, and gave up on the loop portion of the trail altogether.

I certainly had caregiving moments when I felt that I was forging my way through without a clear path. I was going to do it by myself, so help me. I might have a little guidance from a book or an internet search, but by God, I knew my husband, I thought that I knew Alzheimer's disease, and I was going to get it right.

One example of my caregiving floundering, and there were many, was when Harvey showed me a ball of poop in his hand, his eyebrows raised in question about what to do. Well, I knew what to do. You don't hold nasty poop in your hand! I grabbed him by the wrist and made him drop it in the toilet. Then, still holding him by the wrist, I tried to force him to wash his hands. With his free hand, he then grasped my wrist that was holding his, essentially locking us together. Harvey was much stronger than I was, and there was no way that I was going to win this battle. So I relented, and left the situation. Breathing deeply, I was able to calm myself down enough to think of another tactic. By the time I returned, he and I were both calm. I placed my palms over the backs of his hands, and we washed up.

Sometimes with caregiving or with life, you will find yourself lost deep in the woods, trying to make your own way through. It's important to know when to say *when*, give up, and make your way back to a familiar path. Only then can you breathe deeply and look for an easier way forward.

With grief, there was certainly some stumbling around in the dark. Or, rather, lying on my sofa in the dark, crying or staring into space. But my life had to continue. My daughters and my patients needed me. Being needed helped to lift me out of myself and my sorrow. Too, by returning to familiar daily routines—showering, breakfast, seeing patients at the clinic, cooking dinner—I could get through those early days. Patients allowed me to grieve, as together we shared our loss of "Dr. Harvey." On the weekends, returning to familiar trails helped bring me back to myself as my attention focused on what I was seeing and hearing rather than how I was feeling. And returning to community, feeling their compassion for me in warm hugs and thoughtful gestures—cards, calls, meals—confirmed that I was not alone.

IT'S ONLY WATER

I cannot plan my hikes around the weather when I travel with a group. We hike no matter the rain or cold or heat. We are on a schedule, and no allowances are made for comfort. If the weather is dangerous, our leaders capitulate and come up with other plans, but usually, we hike on.

This has made me a bit more flexible when it comes to hiking in all kinds of weather. If I can trek along in cold, blowing rain in Switzerland, what's a little drizzle? I have the luxury at home to schedule my walks and hikes, but when I am away, I want to take advantage of my time in the different location.

One autumn day in north Georgia, for example, the forecast called for rain in the morning, then clearing with a high of fifty-five degrees, though cloudy. Perfect hiking weather. So, I planned to stay in and do some work, then head out for lunch, then a hike, followed by a beer at a local brewery. I guess that I am still a bit rigid, because, by golly, that was the plan, so I stuck with it, even though it was raining throughout lunch and while on my drive to the trail I had picked. It was still misting when I pulled into the parking area.

"Oh, well. It's only water, and I have my rain jacket with its hood and my waterproof boots," I told myself.

It was just past peak autumn leaf season, but still pretty enough. The most colorful leaves littered the trail and the forest floor, and the drizzle caused them to glisten and shine. The deep forest is still peaceful and life-giving in the rain, and my spirits soared as they always do whenever I step into the woods on a sparsely populated trail.

Isn't this a bit like our lives? We can make plans, and decide the best timing for certain events, but in the end, we take what we get. There is no certainty that our plans will carry out the way we want, but we go forward nonetheless. We have to. Even if it's raining and chilly.

Maybe we plan to retire at a certain age, but circumstances make that goal impossible. Maybe we decide that we want to start a family at a certain age, but it just never happens. Maybe a long-awaited vacation is canceled due to a death in the family. Maybe we plan to buy a new house in the coming months, but the interest rates shoot up.

Major and minor events crop up and destroy the best-laid plans all the time. We can't change the weather, we can only change how we respond to it. We have to be flexible enough to pivot and go with whatever presents itself. Being mad, raging about our unfair fate, or sinking into despair does not change the situation. These are often valid emotional responses, though, and shouldn't be ignored, but processed.

Yes, plans are fine, as far as you can rely on them. But bending with whatever the Universe throws at us takes adaptability, resilience, and a positive attitude. Because just stepping outside of the situation and breathing may be all we can do, and it may be just what we need to do so that we can regard that disrupted plan more clearly. It's only water after all.

Some of the most intense preparation I went through was before ascending Mount Kilimanjaro. In advance, the leaders provided our group with a training schedule that involved strength, endurance, and hiking with full daypacks and lots of elevation gain. I was unable to hit all the goals, but I was close. It felt like this training schedule was for younger people with younger knees. And, the training didn't include high altitudes, which, of course, are nonexistent at home in Alabama anyway. The summit of Kilimanjaro is just over 19,000 feet. The contiguous United States has peaks that reach just over 14,000 feet. Just to get a taste of what it would feel like for our bodies to be at these heights, I, and the two friends who trekked with me, flew to Colorado to experience the thin air.

We spent two days hiking challenging trails at lower altitudes of about 7,000 feet. Then we hiked a trail that took us from 12,000 feet elevation to 13,220 feet over the course of just under two miles, and with an aggregate elevation gain of 1,555 feet. The longest, and steepest, section of the trail was at the start, and it was daunting to see the narrow path as it ascended, then followed the ridge of the mountain to reach its crest. We could see tiny ant-sized hikers farther up the trail.

We felt the impact of the thin air fairly quickly, our breaths coming faster as we climbed the slope. We climbed about one hundred feet before having to stop to catch our breath. It didn't take long to recover, usually less than a minute, then we were back on our way. It certainly helped to slow down and just place one foot in front of the other as we made our slow, dogged progress. It was a little disheartening to have people pass us as they seemed to scamper ahead. However, we realized they were all much younger than we were. We saw one, maybe two people on the trail that appeared to be of our advanced years.

What really showed our age was the descent. Old knees do not skip down steep slopes. It was a slow, careful creep, using our trusty trekking poles. When the trail was wide enough, I employed the downhill skiing technique of crossing from one side to the other.

So we learned a lot on that foray onto a high-altitude Colorado trail. The air is thin up there, the elevation stealing your breath. We are no longer young, but we have endurance and fortitude to press on. Slowing down and taking it one step at a time was the best option. Keeping our eyes on the present so as not to be overwhelmed by what we needed to accomplish was imperative.

All this training reminded me that we cannot fully train for all that life throws at us. Hopefully, our parents taught us how to be moral persons and prepared us for independence. College gave some of us wings to try out that independence and graduate school trained some of us in our professions. But really, we cannot fully train to be a successful human being in the world because we cannot anticipate all that might come our way. We may have the grounding and life skills to face our futures, but not specific knowledge on how to surmount particular challenges.

Yes, we have to make plans for the future. We cannot just fly by the seat of our pants all the time. But living for the future and planning for outcomes we desire can only go so far. All it takes is one bump in the road—one unexpected diagnosis, one random car accident, one bad decision—and all the plans in the world will fail us.

When our plans fall apart, and we are confronted with a present that we didn't see coming, we have to lean into our prior training—patience, endurance, fortitude, optimism—in order to learn to accept it, even if it means we go through a grief process for the future we thought was ours. When we find ourselves on an unexpected path, our life's plan upturned, it is normal and natural to grieve the loss of *normal*, and what we thought *normal* would be. All the experiences from our past have taught us how to, or how not to, react. Something as simple as failing a test that I should have aced taught me that I didn't have to give up, that I could still work to improve my grade (and that failing a test didn't mean that I was a failure). Owning a mistake I made in parenting taught me that I would not be perfect in caregiving. Putting my head down and pushing through rough patches of residency training taught me that I had endurance and persistence.

One week in early May, I had another experience of literally putting my head down and pushing through. It was on the same driving and hiking trip along the Blue Ridge Parkway in North Carolina where I got lost; I picked a new hike to Crabtree Falls. It was a loop trail, my favorite kind, and if all went well, I would descend to the falls, then back up and out, following a stream. The falls were beautiful, and I lingered there, and breathed, and took photographs. A gentle rain made its way through the forest canopy soon after I left the falls to complete the trail's loop. I could hear distant thunder. *How pleasant*, I thought. Then the rain became a very heavy downpour, and I was quickly soaked. Not so pleasant. But what could I do? There were no porches to shelter under. I had to stick it out. Walking as fast as I could up the trail, I kept my head down and forged on.

The trail emerged into a campground, and I spied a bathhouse. Finally, a respite from the torrent. But there was another hiker already there. I wondered if I should just keep going and bypass the chance to shelter, or if I should hunker down with a stranger in the men's room. I chose the latter.

My fellow storm weatherer was a photographer as well as a hiker, and we chatted amiably until the rain relented. Our short time together in the restroom was quite nice, and it made me wonder why I had even contemplated trudging on in the rain instead of stopping. Was it because I wanted to believe I could do this by myself? That I was self-sufficient enough to go it alone?

Sometimes life sends us storms. We can seek shelter in the company of others, or in solitude with the Divine. Sometimes there is no shelter available, and we must just carry on, plunging ahead and making a path on our own, hopefully while recognizing that the Divine is always with us.

The storm of Harvey's illness and his death afforded me with several opportunities for both options. When I could, I chose to bring others on board to help me ride out the storm. They brought companionship and encouragement. Other times, there was nothing to do except to keep moving forward. If I was truly awake to the moment, I would stop, take a deep breath, or several, and then I could sense that I had the strength to put my head down and get the job done. Because the Divine is always walking alongside me.

And magic truly happens when a painful experience offers some unexpected gifts, just like the lovely conversation with the photographer sheltering with me in the men's room. Looking back on Harvey's time with Alzheimer's disease, there were some gifts. As expressed in the poem that begins this section, by meeting him exactly where he was, I could loosen up in my role as caregiver and play with him as if we were children. Too, I learned to just be in the moment with him, sitting quietly together. There can be unexpected enjoyment even on an unexpected rocky journey.

CHAPTER 5

Time Travel

It can be mind-bending to explore the idea of time travel or nonlinear time. Books and movies are replete with this conceit. The closest I've come to traveling back in time was on that mountain road during the pandemic (as discussed in the introduction), experiencing all four seasons within a thirty-minute period—early summer at the base transitioning into full winter at the summit.

When I was five years old, my best friend told me that she was getting younger instead of older with time. I was amazed that she had already experienced adulthood, and that we were just crossing paths on her way to infancy. And I really believed her. When I told my mother about this astounding phenomenon, she scoffed. Soon after, my friend moved to a new city, and I was able to hold on to that fantasy for several years. When I saw the movie *The Curious Case of Benjamin Button*, that memory reappeared, and I marveled at the imagination my young friend had and at my child-self's ability to believe the possibility.

Then I watched Harvey travel back in time as his Alzheimer's disease progressed. Obviously, it wasn't as quick as my mountain climb, and it was faster than Benjamin Button's time travel, but over the eight years of his disease, I watched Harvey regress from adult, to adolescent, to child, to infant.

When I found the Functional Assessment Staging Test (FAST) online, with its detailed descriptions of each stage and substage of Alzheimer's disease, I was buoyed with this new knowledge. But what really caught my attention was the scale's duration of each of the stages and age equivalents in each stage. It clicked. Someone had actually done the research to assign an approximate chronologic age to each of the seven stages and substages of Alzheimer's disease.

It really helped me to interact with Harvey more appropriately when I made the realization that he had the mind of a child, or a toddler, or an infant. I was careful not to infantilize him, but I could play with him as if he were a child, shooting hoops, playing catch, or batting balloons. If I spoke to him in simple language, he could better understand me. I was meeting him where he was on his journey back in time.

Unlike Benjamin Button, whose body aged in reverse, it is only the cognitive abilities of a person living with Alzheimer's that are reversing. When I realized that truth, I could better appreciate the beauty of the springtime of childhood in which Harvey was living.

The world that Harvey embodied before was quiet, reflective, thoughtful, and responsible. Harvey's world after became confused, sweet, chaotic, and reactive. His world didn't change overnight. It shifted gradually, some characteristics lingering longer than others, morphing almost imperceptibly, like the lengthening of darkness as winter approaches. Because my memory was intact, and his was not, I could see the changes, where he could not always comprehend what was happening. Because I am a physician, I tended to watch the changes clinically, ticking off which areas of the brain were systematically affected: memory, language, reasoning, visual-spatial.

But it was a strange world for me to enter as a loving spouse. It was sometimes easier to be a clinician and caregiver than a wife. Although I still loved my husband, he was wandering further away from the man I had loved for over twenty years and toward someone unrecognizable to me.

The common approach to dementia caregiving thirty years ago was to reorient the patient to reality. That only led to confusion and frustration for the person living with dementia, and, in turn, to frustration on the part of the caregiver. A person living with dementia cannot understand reality, and it does no good to correct them. You must enter their world and try to see reality from their point of view, which was the approach at the time Harvey and I were navigating the disease. But it's easier said than done.

After one appointment with Harvey's neurologist, I checked the clinical note on the portal and read the doctor's description of Harvey as "childlike" in demeanor. And he was. He was friendly, eager to please, and agreeable. He was like a ten-year-old boy. If the physician saw him this way, maybe I could too. When I looked at my husband through this lens, I began to step away from my role of life mate and became his playmate. We would never be equal partners again, but we could be together on a different playing field. It was just the perspective I needed in this ever-shifting world of dementia.

As the disease progressed, I couldn't expect him to continue his usual household tasks, just as I wouldn't expect a five-year-old to do laundry. But I could play with him as if he were a five-year-old boy. I entered his world—a world where there were fewer and simpler words, where colors and shapes might be more exciting than the story, where affection was found in holding hands, hugs, and a kiss on the cheek. We played catch, danced to the radio, and belted out the choruses of his favorite Jimmy Buffett songs. I read him stories, using my best silly voices.

In the last two years of Harvey's life, the song "If You're Happy and You Know It" became one of our favorite activities. He couldn't sing with me, but his face lit up, and he clapped at the appropriate places. With time, those claps became a little off-beat, and then there was no clapping, yet his face still lit up. In his last months, Harvey's face no longer brightened on hearing our songs, but I still softly sang to him while I fed him, or combed his hair, or held his hand, bringing us together into the world he then inhabited.

I never knew Harvey when he was a child, but I was privileged to know him as a fully embodied human being in all his other worlds, and maybe I even got to glimpse the child he had been. Isn't this what we desire most of those closest to us—to journey through the world, whatever world that is, meeting each other exactly where we are?

THE MOMENT IS NOW

If traveling back in time with Harvey was the best way that I could connect with him, living fully in the moment was another way I coped. Because "the moment" was the only place he could be, joining him there helped me and encouraged mindfulness. Learning to be in the moment in the midst of upheaval and change stabilized me and gave me the courage to move forward. I was going to have to learn to surf the waves of Alzheimer's, because I knew it could capsize us if I didn't.

I've never learned to surf, and the one time I tried, I ended up dislocating my shoulder, but I imagine that surfing is one of the most mindful activities you can do. All your concentration must be centered on your body, your balance, and your connection with the wave. You cannot think of anything else. Your mind can be nowhere else. You are only present.

Practicing mindfulness is a way to metaphorically surf the waves of many of life's challenges. When I struggled to juggle all my added responsibilities, keeping all those plates spinning, donning a different hat almost minute to minute, if I gave myself time to just breathe, I could relax a bit and be more effective. When I gave in to the moment and accepted Harvey exactly as he was, not as he had been or as he should have been, but as he was with all the childlike wonder, confusion, and dependency, I was practicing mindfulness by being fully present.

It's all very well and good to extol the virtues of living in the moment, taking one step at a time. Not everyone is naturally geared that way, though. Most of us seem to be more inclined toward one of three time orientations—the past, the present, or the future. All three are important, of course, but our personalities seem to prefer one mode over the others. None of them are bad, it's just not a good idea to fixate on one over the other two. A healthy balance of the three is ideal. If we don't acknowledge where we have been, we might lose our perspective of where we have come from and what has shaped us. Concentrating only on the here and now can cause us not only to lose sight of our past, but to fail to plan and dream of a future. If we are always looking forward or backward, we may miss the marvel that is right in front of us.

I am mostly present oriented, but future orientation is a close second. I have to remind myself of the importance of the past. It helps me to acknowledge all that has come before, and keeps me from making the same mistakes.

Hiking is a good illustration. I love to research and plan for future adventures. While on the trail, I fully immerse myself in the present. And reviewing my photographs and writing about the hike later helps me appreciate all that I experienced. While I'm hiking, especially if it's a narrow path or uneven terrain, I have to keep my eyes on the ground in front of me. That's when I spot tiny insects, flowers, or interesting rocks. Every now and then I'll see a turtle, a toad, or another unexpected animal. This is my "present mind." Even while on the trail, attending to the ground at my feet, I do look ahead to see where the trail is heading, scanning for obstacles and a trail blaze. I also like to turn around occasionally to see what the trail looks like from that perspective—how steep the ascent or descent was, for example. If I keep my eyes trained only on the trail, I miss things. Important things.

I once found myself within a cloud on a trail in Tennessee, only able to see a few yards into the distance. The trail was actually a rocky streambed, and because of the drizzle and fine mist, there was running water in places. I had to watch my footing the entire way, keeping my eyes glued to my feet so that I could precisely plan each step—onto a rock or solid ground, and not directly into the water. The trail supposedly ended at a meadow with a view, but because the fog was so dense, I could see neither.

From the meadow, I was supposed to pick up another trail. I skirted the periphery of the clearing, looking for a trail marker in the heavy mist, but couldn't find it. I eventually gave up and turned back down the streambed/trail. I could have used my hiking app to locate the new trail, but I was already cold and wet, my spirits dampened. I could no longer see a future. And because of what I learned from this experience, I planned my next hike to better match the weather.

On another hike at Ruffner Mountain, one of the parks within the city limits of Birmingham, I was watching the path in front of me for roots and rocks. I stopped to examine a red-capped mushroom nestled among woodland phlox. When it was time to continue on, and wanting to see where I was on the trail, I looked up and saw our city skyline peeking through some branches. I had chosen just the right moment to check the trail ahead (or the moment had chosen *me*). Had I glanced up just a step before or after, I would have missed it.

When Harvey was living with Alzheimer's disease, his time orientation had to be in the present, and that necessitated my orientation match his when I wanted to connect with him. I had to deal with what was directly in front of me at the time. Now, at this point in time, I can see that this was a gift. My propensity of looking to the future did help me plan ahead by tentatively looking into possible scenarios. As I've said, past orientation is my weakest way of dealing with time, and it became even weaker during Harvey's illness. I just did not want to look back. It made me too sad to think about all that we had lost. Only after his passing was I able to process what had happened.

And now? I still prefer to live in the moment, doing what needs to be done, appreciating what is currently happening. Writing, editing, preparing, and giving presentations remind me of all that has happened. As much as I might want to put it all behind me, it is a part of who I am.

But the future is beckoning, gently calling me to new things. Making new travel plans is exciting, but that's not "the future." I have to heed the voice that is urging me forward toward whatever is next for me. Although I have some hints, I just don't yet know exactly where it is calling me. I will let the moment choose me.

MINDFULNESS AND BREATH

In the Gospels, one of my favorite stories is of Jesus calming the Sea of Galilee when a storm arose. He and his disciples had boarded a boat to escape the crowds, then the storm developed, frightening the disciples while Jesus slept. They woke him as their terror increased, and Jesus rebuked them for their fear, then commanded the waves to dissipate. While this story is often offered as proof of Jesus as a miracle worker, like many of the gospel stories, a deeper meaning can be found. One such interpretation may be that when we put our trust in the Divine and stop acting out of our anxieties, or trying to control our circumstances, life's storms can lessen—or at least seem less severe.

Jesus calmed the waves for his disciples and eased their fears, but sometimes the waves cannot be stilled. They will just keep coming. Learning to ride them, keeping your balance in the middle of the storm, is often miracle enough.

As a practice of being fully present in the moment, mindfulness can be utilized all the time. It doesn't have to wait until you're sitting on the meditation cushion. The most mindful activity I've encountered was driving the Tail of the Dragon from Tennessee into North Carolina. Its official designation is US Highway 129, and it consists of eleven miles and 318 curves, many of them named. Since I purchased a Mazda Miata, I had been told countless times that I needed to drive this road. It is a destination for motorcycle and sports car drivers.

And that is exactly who I encountered on my drive. No RVs, big rigs, or bicycles were to be seen. There were Harley stores and motorcycle hangouts at both ends of this segment of highway. It felt as if I were entering an amusement park for vehicles—a roller coaster for those of us with fun-to-drive wheels.

I was a little intimidated to enter the Tail of the Dragon because of its reputation. But enter I did. I really can't tell you much about the specifics of my drive. I don't know the elevation change, but I know that I ascended into the mountains, then dropped back down. I couldn't begin to tell you about any particular curve or how I tackled each one. I was totally immersed in the driving experience. Every nerve ending in my body was honed to the task. I was fully engaged—with my mind, my eyes, my ears, and my sense of location in space. I was aware of my surroundings only as they related to the road and the car. I remember flashes of wildflowers and the occasional sign. And the professional photographers set up strategically, with their huge camera lenses trained on me and my car.

It sounds clichéd, but I felt merged with my tiny toy car as I maneuvered the turns and banks of the Tail of the Dragon. My instincts to accelerate, brake, or make fine steering adjustments for an approaching turn were fully present. There was no time for fear or anxiety. I could only drive. It was an intense experience, but I reveled in the sensation of being so attuned to this one task. Here was mindfulness on steroids.

Sometimes our lives move fast, with changes coming at us quickly. We can't always slow down. What if we lived mindfully in times like this? Completely aware of our immediate surroundings, making small adjustments when life throws us a curve. So focused on and attentive to our current situation that our instincts operate precisely. What if we were so attuned to our circumstances, and those people around us, that we felt merged with them—not in a controlling manner, but by a meshing of our collective goals?

I felt something akin to this instinctual adjusting as I made big life decisions, such as those about Harvey's care, as well as my plans to move to a new house and my offer to babysit my first grandchild. Huge changes in my life cropped up seemingly overnight, and my gut reactions took over, and I mostly knew what needed to be done in those situations. And they were the right decisions. There isn't always time to deliberate or make a list of pros and cons. Each of these three life decisions also involved others, and making the right decision took into account what was best for all of us—Harvey, me, my daughters, and my grandchild.

Sometimes finding the flow state of mindfulness is fast—like riding the Tail of the Dragon. But it can be slow too. Rather than setting the metaphorical cruise control on the six-lane freeway of life, what if we took the back roads and concentrated all our attention on the details of our one singular, precious life? Getting from point A to point B is much more interesting if we are engaged and alert, even if we are moving very quickly.

My hiking style, especially when I hike alone, is to move fast, then pause to catch my breath when the need arises. I like to monitor my heart rate, and I've noticed that when it reaches about 140 beats per minute, I am working hard. At 150 I usually choose to take a break, watch my heart rate, and head back up the trail once it reaches 120. This is not what the experts recommend; it's just my way. Part of that is a desire for exercise, but I am aware that with this style of hiking, I will miss things on the trail—small insects and other animals, new-to-me wildflowers, tiny mushrooms.

The style of hiking on Mount Kilimanjaro is *pole pole* (poh'-lay poh'-lay), or "slowly slowly." I knew this going in, and I knew it would be difficult for me. I also knew that we were supposed to stay together as a group. I was worried that I would become frustrated with the pace, so I mentally prepared myself to just go with this particular flow.

What I didn't count on was the steep incline of the terrain, even right at the beginning. While mentally I knew that we would gain four thousand feet over seven miles on the first day, I just didn't have any concept of what that elevation gain would look or feel like. The most elevation gain I can achieve in Alabama is about two thousand feet over fourteen miles or so.

So up we went, using pole pole pace. I didn't break a sweat, and my heart rate stayed below 120. We took rare breaks for water, but because I was using a hydration system as part of my daypack, sipping along the way, I didn't even need those. I wasn't tired except for my upper back because of the weight of my pack. I was amazed. If I had done my usual pace of go fast then take a break, it would have taken me much longer to cover those seven miles.

As we climbed into ever-higher altitudes, pole pole became even more important. One day, about halfway in, our group decided to be silent for the first thirty minutes of our hike. I was directly behind our guide, and I began to pay attention to his gait. Pole pole for me looked like step, pause, step, pause, step, and so on. The guide's movements, on the other hand, were slow and fluid, almost like a dance. He would pick up one foot, slowly move it forward, then place weight on it, over and over again. I tried to mimic him, but it was difficult as I was essentially trying to balance on one foot for a longer period of time than usual. I eventually got the hang of it. I don't know if there is any advantage of the guide's pole pole over mine, but it was beautiful to watch and fun to try. And it made me become more aware and alert to each step.

Of course, the lesson here is an old one. I'm sure you've heard the story of the tortoise and the hare! There is a lot that I could say about slowing down, taking one step at a time, but not much that hasn't already been said by people much wiser than I. However, I need to hear those lessons often. I need to focus on cultivating mindfulness; it doesn't come naturally to me. I do tend to rush through life without treasuring moments as they occur. Or look ahead to what the future may hold while ignoring what's right in front of me. Or rushing to finish a goal, only to have to pause to rest and reassess for a moment because I got too caught up in the forward movement.

Large, complicated goals should be addressed step by step, looking at the trees along the way, and not obsessing about the forest or the endgame. On Kilimanjaro, our head guide even warned us not to think ahead to summit day because we would fill our brains with anxiety and miss the beauty of each day as it presented itself. And while summiting was certainly a bucket-list feat, the small moments of the journey are what I remember best now.

Hand in hand with mindfulness goes breathing. Breathing just comes naturally to us. We don't even have to think about it. It's an automatic function our bodies perform to keep us alive. But it's also one of only two bodily functions that we can override. We can choose to hold our breath or breathe faster. Some people can control their heart rate and blood pressure with training and practice, but not to the degree that we can all easily achieve with our lungs. (And what's the other automatic function that we can overrule? Blinking!)

The exchange of carbon dioxide for oxygen in our animal bodies is reversed in an opposite exchange of these gases in plants—a beautiful example of reciprocity. Humans, and all animals, need oxygen to survive. All the cells in our bodies require oxygen to produce energy, and that energy is what fuels all the functions (cardiac, digestion, muscular, etc.) that we take for granted. As one ascends into higher altitudes, the oxygen content in the air decreases, as does the ambient air pressure. Both are factors in why it is so much harder to breathe at extremely high altitudes.

Because the energy demands of elite athletes are greater than yours or mine, there are breathing techniques that they can engage in to maximize the exchange of oxygen and carbon dioxide. The most basic technique is belly breathing. At rest, we normally breathe with just our chests, which controls the top-most portion of our lungs. If we breathe with our bellies, we engage our diaphragms and pull air into the lower portion of our lungs, which can carry substantially more air than the upper sections. So athletes who employ the belly breath regularly will necessarily pull in more oxygen and let out more carbon dioxide. Not that I am an elite athlete, but this breathing technique works at high altitudes, where the oxygen content is lower, to the same effect.

Another breathing technique that I learned while on Kilimanjaro was the "pressure breath." In addition to breathing with the diaphragm, one adds forceful expirations. This is best achieved by pursing the lips, puffing out the cheeks, and pretending to blow through a straw. This increases the air pressure in the lungs, countering the low ambient pressure at high altitudes, and allowing more efficient gas exchange to occur.

By taking into account the lower air pressure, and applying this breathing technique, what once was unbalanced becomes balanced. While hiking at extreme altitude, I corrected the shortcomings of the lack of pressure by supplying and increasing my own. And isn't this how we should move in the world? Taking a sabbatical, even for just a day, when we are overstressed. Getting together with a friend after spending a lot of time with just ourselves. Planning a date with our spouse when we realize we have taken the partnership for granted. When we are mindful of the imbalances in our lives, it pays to correct them with countermeasures.

Paying attention to my breath, my pace, and my climbing technique took a lot of mental awareness. By concentrating on all these aspects of high-altitude hiking, my mind was occupied and couldn't focus as much on my discomfort or fatigue. I could easily have gotten stuck into a thought rut: *This is so hard. I can't do this. When is the next break?* But by bringing my brain back to my breath, I tuned out that voice. When we pay attention to how we move in the world, we necessarily become more aware of our surroundings and how we interact with them.

Beyond helping out in athletic situations, breath work, any practice of manipulation of the breath, is a common form of meditation that has been shown to reduce stress and improve mental health. By concentrating on our breath, we can quiet the chatter in our mind and become more attuned to the world around us. But more than that, studies have shown that slowing your breath or employing the belly breath actually promotes changes in your autonomic and central nervous systems, modifying activities in the heart and in the brain in positive, verifiable, and quantifiable ways.

There are several techniques that you can employ, belly breathing being one. My favorite is the box breath, or loop breath. In my mind's eye, I envision a square, and as I inhale on a count of four or five, I move up one side. Then I hold my breath for another count of four or five as my mind crosses the top of the box. An exhalation down the opposite side and another breath hold across the bottom completes one cycle. I can literally feel myself becoming more calm when taking the time to do this work.

I would routinely pause outside a patient's door before entering, taking about thirty seconds of simple deep breathing, maybe not the box breath per se. In a busy family medicine practice, I would sometimes feel overly rushed to see all the patients that needed to be seen in a timely manner. Just that little bit of a pause and deep breaths would clear my mind, and calm and center me. My patients deserved the best me that I could present, and this was one tool that helped me deliver that care.

I employed breathing techniques when caring for Harvey too. In the situation I previously described of him holding poop in his hand, I stepped away to calm myself with deep breaths before I attempted another avenue to direct him. It happened less frequently, but when Harvey became agitated, if I could get him to do some breath work, taking slow, deep breaths, sometimes that would break his resistance to care. Because we would be doing it together, it certainly worked to calm me, and therefore, my steady presence could be reflected back to him.

And in that moment, breathing together or separately, no other thoughts can intrude. You can only be in the moment, following your breath.

CHAPTER 6

From Fear to Compassion

The Sipsey Wilderness is a pristine forest in northwest Alabama. Deep canyons formed by creeks and rivers over eons have protected this area from being developed. If I wanted to explain the color green to someone, the Sipsey would be my definition. Multiple hues of verdant plant life exist there, nestled in the deep shade of the forest.

I had hiked and camped there before, years ago with Harvey and some friends, then later with our daughters. I hadn't been back until a couple of years ago, solo, when I camped in a campground and made day hikes. The area had no cellular service, so before I left home, and using my trusty hiking app, I downloaded trails that looked promising, then updated my family with each hike I took.

The first trail was called Shangri-La, a promising name for a trail if ever there was one. The description promised a haven with a waterfall cascading into a quiet pool at its end. I was hooked. Well, the trail ended up being only a suggestion.

There were no trail blazes, nothing. The hiking app tracks my location on the downloaded map, so using my cell phone as a compass of sorts, I trekked through underbrush, down slippery mud banks, and crossed a creek, finally reaching the destination. It was just as heavenly as described and completely worth the trouble!

The second trail I chose was Little Ugly Creek and Deer Skull Falls, not a very encouraging name for a trail, and quite the contrast in name to Shangri-La. This one started with the good potential of a marked path, but it quickly turned into just a hint. Using the app again, I navigated steep walls, crossed the "ugly creek" multiple times, and walked along a very narrow portion at the edge of the canyon. I kept envisioning snakes or a fall, then pushed them out of my mind, and hiked on. I never saw a deer skull, and the creek was indeed ugly. As an aside, I recently looked up this trail on the hiking app and read a review from someone who had to be airlifted out after sustaining a broken leg. I won't be back.

The third hike was along Borden Creek. I chose it because it actually looked to be a real trail, with its trailhead at a substantial parking lot. A flat, well-traveled path followed the course of the creek. There was no chance of a fall, but I did come upon a snake lying across the trail, which stopped me short until I could get a better look to see that it was not of the venomous variety. At another spot, an opossum ambled along a portion of the trail just in front of me. It had rained recently, and there were vast crops of mushrooms. Several umbrella magnolias and hemlocks provided shade, and a steep rock cliff with outcrops, trickling waterfalls, and shallow caves was on my right.

The trail seemed to stop abruptly at a giant boulder that was right at the creek's edge. I couldn't go around it. I decided to try to climb over it, but that was not possible either. I was about to give up and turn back when I noticed an opening in the rock. It was pitch black, but when I bent over and walked in, I could see daylight far to my left. As my eyes adjusted to the gloom inside this opening, I could make out a passage through the boulder. Maybe this was the trail? I had to take off my daypack and carry it in front of myself, hunched over, and still my shoulders scraped the walls as I inched along toward the light at the other end. When I emerged, I could tell immediately that this was indeed the continuation of the trail.

I must have missed a description of this scary tunnel on my hiking app, because when I told a friend about my adventure, he said, "Oh, Fat Man's Squeeze. That's a really fun hike," as if this was a well-known feature. Had I known about it beforehand, I wouldn't have had near as much fear about entering that dark passage, but I'm proud of myself for pushing down my apprehension and pushing on toward the light.

Sometimes the only way forward is through a dark fear. But fear can hold us back from realizing many of life's treasures—a seemingly impossible goal, a new adventure, a deepening friendship. It can teach you things about yourself as well.

RELEASING FEAR

A trip to the Galápagos Islands taught me more about fear and the beauty of shedding it. My adventure began when my father asked me to consider doing this trip together. I had always wanted to visit the Galápagos and thought I would eventually either make the trip solo, or else ask a girlfriend to go with me. I had no idea that my father was interested, but he told me that the Galápagos was the only place he had any desire to visit, and that at the age of eighty-eight, he knew he better get busy. After contemplating his offer for about two minutes, I accepted.

So not only did I get to experience this magical place, a

zoo without cages and an aquarium without glass walls, but I got to experience it with my father. If this was the only place on earth to which he wanted to transplant his body and spirit, what a privilege it would be for me to accompany him.

One of the most arresting features on the Galápagos Islands is the docile nature of the animals there. I was aware of this fact and assumed that the animals are unafraid of humans because we had been visiting them for so long that they had lost their fear of us. That's just not the case. Rather, for millennia, they had no reason to be scared of us, or of any other creatures. In fact, the largest land and air predator is the small Galápagos hawk. There was and is no need to have a fight-or-flight reaction to possible predators, including humans.

Humans came late to the scene on the Galápagos, just under five hundred years ago, and our presence there has been spotty. Those earliest visitors noted that the animals had no fear of them, thus the nickname, the Enchanted Islands. Now that the islands are protected, there is even less of a reason for the indigenous inhabitants to be afraid of us. We are just those creatures with two legs that come to look at them.

Birds were on full display in the Galápagos Islands. And when I say "full display," I don't just mean there were lots of birds. I mean that it felt as if they were actually displaying themselves for us. The birds were completely indifferent to us; we could walk right up to within the prescribed six feet, and they didn't fly away or even flinch. They just went about the business of being birds—building nests, feeding their chicks, performing mating rituals, or incubating their eggs.

The birds there, just being birds, reminded me that life can be simpler when we are just ourselves. When we resist the instinct to hide parts of ourselves, our true essences can shine. When we don't flee from the scrutiny of others, we can go about the business of living our lives. When we are unabashedly ourselves, our individual beauty is apparent.

What if we take a cue from the birds and other animals on the Galápagos Islands and live without fear? And I don't mean fear of snakes, spiders, heights, or other phobias. But rather, an attitude of fearlessness, approaching life without trepidation, as if something exciting is always around the corner.

Now, obviously a certain amount of fear is healthy. I'm not advocating unbuckling your seat belt or jumping out of an airplane without a parachute. Insurance policies have their place. Saving for the future is prudent. I'm speaking more about the fear that holds us back from gaining our true potential. Fear of failure will certainly hold us back from achieving what we desire, but if we don't try, we will necessarily fail. We will never gain an insight into what we are capable of if we remain idle in the face of a challenge. What about fear of success? Is that even a thing? Sure it is. If we do something really well, we may fear that we will be called upon to repeat that success. We risk developing impostor syndrome if others think we are more expert than we view ourselves to be.

Living without fear in our relationships leads to vulnerability and honesty and deep connection. Feeling afraid keeps us from fully engaging. We don't want to be hurt or disappointed. But in the end, isn't it worth it? Isn't the chance of finding a new friend or a deepening connection with a loved one more satisfying than wondering, *What if*?

Then there is the fear of the unknown. How best to embrace bravery in these situations? Researching something may make us more comfortable before jumping, but sometimes we are called upon to just jump. I sometimes like to be surprised, especially if I feel that the odds are in favor of it being a good surprise. I come up against this sentiment most often when traveling. For two summers in a row, I jumped at experiences of hiking in Europe. I jumped because the opportunity was too hard to resist. I actually did very little research into these two trekking adventures. I just went with my gut because they sounded so appealing and exciting. And they were wonderful trips, worth any amount of apprehension I might have had.

If we live our lives in fear, we aren't really living. Sometimes we just need to put down the fear and leap.

I have one more story that illustrates releasing fear. There is a tree with a large hole in its trunk on one of my favorite hikes. My poem "Alzheimer's Beautiful Scars" uses this tree for its inspiration. It sits on the bank of a small stream that the hiking trail runs alongside. The main trail makes a turn away from the creek before it gets to the tree. If I remember in time, I will veer off the trail to follow the stream so that I can see "my" tree again.

This is not a very big tree aboveground, but its visible root system is massive. Maybe that's just because it is so visible. If it was all underground, as most tree roots are, it would be just as massive, just unseen. But this tree's roots are clinging to the bank, sprawling out laterally in both directions, and reaching into the stream itself. It's as if the tree is holding on to the riverbank, clawing desperately to hang on. I wish I could see what this stream and tree looked like fifty or a hundred years ago. Has the creek been slowly eroding its bank, eating away at the soil that the tree had previously plunged its roots into? It's as if the tree is hanging on to its past—its prior security and depth and source of nourishment.

How like that tree we can be, desperately clinging to the shores of what we know, fearing the unknown. It's our solid ground, our security, and maybe even the source of prior nourishment. It's what we know. So we claw and scrape to continue holding on to this place, this knowing. But if we continue to cling to the past, we can't move forward. Of course, a tree is not meant to move forward; it can only grow upward, dependent on its roots for its place. But humans are meant to move forward.

When we let go of the banks of our knowing and allow

the stream to carry us, we experience new vistas, new landscapes. And I don't mean literally. Our emotional and spiritual landscapes can gain new insights if we loosen our grasp on what we thought we have always known. Falling into the same thought patterns gets us nowhere. There is comfort in familiar internal landscapes, and nostalgia feels nice. For a while. But unrelenting patterns of anxiety, melancholy, and self-doubt afford no new growth, no new way of being.

We cannot live in the past. We have to let go. We may not know where the current will take us, but we trust the Universe to carry us to where we are supposed to go. We must live now. The river of life will flow despite our fears and our efforts to hold on to the shore of our past knowing. The river might even eat away at the bank, forcing us into her flow. We could scrabble and fight to get back to the shore we know. Or we can choose to relax, put our feet in front of us, and let the river move us forward. From the middle of the river, we have the vantage of seeing the shores as we are carried by.

There will be eddies and rocks we have to maneuver around, and there may come floodwaters that swamp us at times. So maybe it's best if we build a boat. A boat made of sturdy, life-sustaining principles—honesty, vulnerability, kindness, integrity. Then we can more securely sail the river of life, letting it take us to our future.

On a recent trip to North Carolina, I wanted to introduce my sister, Andrea, to a hike along a portion of the Appalachian Trail. I picked a section that crossed a nearby highway, making it very accessible. After I parked my car in the small lot adjacent to the two-lane road, we geared up in boots, backpacks, and hiking poles that were stashed in the back of my car. When I turned around, I saw a black bear. It was crossing the highway, heading toward us, not quite at the line that divides the road into opposing lanes. I froze—my usual response—and muttered aloud, "There's a bear." Andrea turned and locked eyes for a fraction of a second with the bear, then it turned and fled the way it had come. We actually heard its claws scrape the guardrail as it clambered over it. The bear was just as scared of us as we were of it!

Another encounter had a similar effect on me, even if it wasn't as terrifying in the end. Returning to my newly acquired lake house alone one day, ten days after I was last there, I found the front door standing wide open. My brain swirled with anxious thoughts: What should I do? Just walk in as if nothing was amiss? Call the police and have them check it out first? Shut and lock the door and leave? I decided to go in. It took all the courage I could muster to enter the house, all the while yelling, "Hello! Anybody here?" The hair on my arms was standing at attention as I continued to shout and check every room. Nothing was disturbed. The TV, the only item of value, was still there. All seemed to be as I had left it. Then I heard a scratching sound. As I turned and crept toward the noise, a small dun-colored bird fluttered out of the laundry closet and tried to fly out of a closed window.

My fear of what might lie on the other side of that open front door evaporated. I had walked through the door into the unknown, but now I was confronted with a fellow creature who was also in foreign territory, and compassion for its plight became stronger than my fear. As I contemplated how to proceed, the bird suddenly flew into another room of the house. I followed it into the small bedroom, then opened one of the windows and left, closing the door behind me. The bird found its way out a few minutes later. What a perfect illustration of compassion overcoming fear. Upon further refection, I realized that when I feel trapped and scared by circumstances, a door just might open for me, if I can truly trust and have compassion for myself.

Of course, wild animals are not the only beings we might be afraid of. I attend a downtown church, where I, and others, regularly have interactions with people experiencing homelessness in the area. My initial reaction in these encounters used to be fear. Who is this person? Do they want to harm me? Their appearance doesn't fit with the environment, and they seem out of place, and therefore, appear a little scary to me. But really, that is just my societal conditioning talking. When fear gives way to compassion, I can interact with them as fellow travelers in this world. We don't know each other's stories, but we don't have to know them to see each other as humans who are all doing the best we can. Feeling compassion for a person experiencing homelessness rather than crossing the street in fear expands our capacity to be truly human. Why not meet their gaze with direct eye contact and smile? Even better, stop to have a conversation.

A healthy guardedness can protect us from stranger danger, and I'm not advocating walking downtown streets alone at night, hitchhiking, or accepting drinks from a stranger. Fear is a healthy response to a situation that feels dangerous. And we each have a different danger meter, I suspect, depending on upbringing, general inclination, and past experiences.

While hiking, I often encounter individuals on the trail, and I've never felt frightened. Sometimes we stop and chat for a bit, mostly we greet each other and keep going. After the hike with the bear encounter, when Andrea and I returned to the parking lot, an older couple was just starting up the trail. We stopped to tell them about the bear. In turn, the woman said, "You know what animal you should be most afraid of in these woods is, don't you?"

"Ticks?" I asked.

"No. Humans."

She then proceeded to tell us about a recent incident of a serial killer who had attacked three people on trails in the area and was eventually caught. I was thrown off guard, having just finished a lovely hike with my sister in early summer—a hike replete with wildflowers, a small waterfall, and stunning overlooks. This woman's comment reminded me that it's not all trees and flowers and vistas. But the bear and this woman's story haven't deterred me from hiking further. I may be more aware of my surroundings now, but I refuse to let fear keep me from the trails.

Our society generally teaches us to be fearful of those who are not like us. We are more comfortable within our community of like-minded people. Extending hospitality toward people whose identities don't overlap our own can take great courage as we push against those societal boundaries. Our instinct may be to shelter with our community. It takes mindfulness to willfully see "the other" with the same type of compassion you would have for those in your circle. We are also taught to be wary of traditions and customs that we don't understand. We think them strange, and we tend to denigrate them and the people that hold to them.

Developing compassion for those not like us takes practice. The first step is self-awareness, becoming alert to those internal alarm bells ringing inside of you signaling fear. When you feel that fear, you can then mindfully stop and examine the source of your fear. Is it logical? What are you actually afraid of? You might also increase your compassion by deliberately expanding your circle and becoming proximate with people you wouldn't regularly associate with. I've experienced many people who, once they got to know someone who they initially thought of as different, reversed course and became champions for their new friends. We can change. We do not have to be fearful of each other's differences.

I used to think that the opposite of fear was courage. But courage is the flip side of fear; it uses the same type of energy. Maybe the opposite of fear is actually peacefulness. Fear has no place when we are in a state of calm acceptance.

COMPASSION FOR THE SELF

Turning fear into compassion for others is a lifelong practice. But what about self-compassion? I've written quite a bit about self-care when one is a caregiver for a loved one. It is so important to take care of oneself in order to be the best provider of care for those we hold most dear. They deserve the best that we can give. How can we give good care if we are not at our best?

This includes caring for our physical, emotional, and spiritual selves. And it's not a selfish thing to do at all. Putting our needs second to our loved ones' may be appropriate at times, but disregarding our personal needs altogether never is.

Self-care is *not* saying "I've had a horrible week, so I deserve to drink this bottle of wine, alone, with a bag of potato chips and a pint of ice cream, in front of the television tonight." That's self-indulgence. We are not actually caring for our bodies, minds, or spirits with these types of actions, we are simply dissociating. Self-care implies taking *good* care of the life that we have been given.

If self-care is an action, then self-compassion is a state of mind that will lead to self-care. While I do think that I practice good self-care most of the time, I am also often my own worst enemy when it comes to self-compassion. Self-compassion involves giving yourself the same respect, care, and loving-kindness that you would give to a good friend. The word *compassion* literally means "suffer with." When encountering a dear friend who is living through a difficult experience, we are moved with compassion. When we see another person or an animal suffering, and we feel empathy for their pain, our hearts are moved, and we want to ease that pain, or at least try to understand it.

Having compassion for another also means offering

understanding and kindness when they fail, or make mistakes, rather than judging them harshly. We wouldn't treat a friend with cruel taunts and criticisms when they make a mistake, so why do we do it to ourselves? We deserve the same compassion that we extend to our friends.

For caregivers, this most often involves not beating ourselves up when we fail to live up to our own goals and standards. Providing care for persons living with dementia is very difficult. Providing perfect care is impossible. I have yet to meet a care partner who filled this role without some missteps. Often our harshest critic is the one that camps out in our brains. If we would not expect perfection from our friends, why do we demand it of ourselves?

I really could be talking to myself here. I regularly beat myself up for not being the caregiver to Harvey that I wanted to be. But I also know that I was doing the best I could with the internal resources that I had. I was better at self-care than I was at self-compassion, though. I followed through on practices and routines that had always brought me happiness, sometimes altering them to fit our new reality. For example, instead of hiding away in my reading nook with a novel, I began to listen to audiobooks. Instead of going to my craft room to play, I taught myself how to knit and crochet so that I could sit with Harvey in the evenings.

Even now, I can be a pretty harsh self-critic, but I'm better, especially without the roles of caregiver and physician. Still, I find myself saying "Stupid!" under my breath when I make a simple mistake. Not very compassionate. I continue my self-care practices, though—walking, hiking, one-on-one time with friends and family—all the things that continue to bring me joy.

Showing compassion toward oneself when faced with shortcomings is a healthy approach. We will make mistakes. Everyone does. Acknowledge it, then be a good friend to yourself, and with compassion, recognize that the situation you are living with is worthy of your own compassion. Be kind to yourself. Offer yourself words of understanding and comfort. Forgive yourself.

If we start with self-compassion, it will ultimately lead to following best practices of self-care, which will lead to having a happier, healthier, more fulfilling, and more whole life.

**

A deep freeze one late December delivered scant snow, a layer of ice, and put me in a holding pattern. It was silent as the world slowly awoke that morning. No birds sang. No squirrels chattered. All God's creatures were hunkered down as temperatures hovered below twenty degrees. I include myself among those hunkered creatures, barely moving all day as I nested in my cozy spot, dressed in pajamas and bathrobe, swaddled in a blanket. Looking out my window high above the street, I could see that the road and the cars were coated in a layer of glossy ice.

The flight of concrete stairs from my house to the street was encased in ice, too, making it hazardous to attempt a descent, so I stayed unmoving all day, reading, and watching the world from my vantage point. It was an unexpected, forced sabbath. I was frozen in, literally and figuratively.

I don't often stop and just keep in a holding pattern all day. There are things that need to be done—groceries to shop for, plants that need tending, clothes that need washing. And there are things that I want to do—meeting a friend for coffee, visiting my parents, playing with my grandchildren. The busyness of life, or the business of life, keeps me moving. Even when I'm in nature, attentive to what the Universe has to teach me, I am usually walking, rarely stopping for any length of time. I do take time during the day, usually in the early morning, to gather myself and my plans, but that involves a lot of mental movement.

That day of ice made me wonder if my busyness was a way to avoid the world, the hard things of the world, or even avoid self-compassion and self-care. Do I close myself off with busyness? Is it self-compassion to stop and take a day away from the everyday hassles and chores?

I have had the experience of being spiritually and emotionally frozen. When life is overwhelming, sometimes I just shut down. Perhaps I use busyness as a means of icing myself in, walling myself off from the world and from myself. It's as if my emotions are encased in ice. It's a defense mechanism I'm sure, a mode of survival. Eventually, though, I will want to escape, break free from the solid immovable ice sculpture I've become. Sometimes it happens unexpectedly. Memories, beauty, and love have a way of warming my heart again, and, with time, thawing occurs. My heart melts in a puddle, all the emotions I had frozen away now oozing out, trickling into all the cracks and crevices of my life.

Other times, it takes effort on my part. When I sense an unease, a disgruntlement with myself, when I realize that I am clinging to a worn-out pattern that doesn't serve me anymore, I often turn inward. If I reach deep into my soul toward the god-spark within, realizing that I am whole and that I am loved as I am, I can rekindle the tiny flame that will melt my heart. And if I can focus on that space within, breathe deeply into my heart, knowing that I am taking in the Divine that is all around with each breath, the warmth of the breath rekindles that spark and takes the chill off.

For only in the deep sense of knowing that we are loved, by the Divine and by our own selves, will our self-compassion thaw our souls.

PART THREE

Coming Home to Myself

ORDINARY DAY

Impossible blue sky
Carries the early morning breeze that
Tickles the hair on my arms.
I inhale with my entire being,
And there—a faint, sweet perfume—
Tea olives, their tiny ivory flowers flavor-
    ing the air.

Awareness of my world, all senses waking
    up

Taking off on an easy run,
I adjust my stride for roots and rocks.
When my heart rate peaks and breath
    becomes labored,
I slow to a walk.

Awareness of the world of my body

Memories of his lean runner's frame
And his fluid, effortless stride
Snake into my brain.

I miss him again for the five thousandth time,
But instead of tears, I smile.

Awareness that the world of grief means there was once great love

Later, playing with my granddaughter,
Rolling on the floor, reading *Goodnight Moon* before bed.
A quarter of her self from me, a quarter from him.
She won't meet him, but she will know him
Through the stories we tell.

Awareness that the world of her future self is rooted in past generations

In bed that night, I fluff my pillow
Turn it over to its cooler side.
I reach for the other pillow, his pillow,
And hold it close to my chest.
Soft light filters through the gauzy curtains,
Dampening the shadows of grief.
Low hum of spring insects serenades me to sleep.

Awareness of the small world of my bedroom

CHAPTER 7

Adapting to Change

We all experience change throughout our lives. The only constant is change. How we deal with it is as individual as we are. Change can be scary or exciting, terrifying or exhilarating, expected or unexpected, sudden or gradual. Change necessarily means we have to adapt to it. If we don't, old ways of living in the world just won't work anymore.

When Harvey was diagnosed with Alzheimer's disease, our individual worlds changed dramatically, and I sometimes went kicking and screaming into that new world. Eventually, I learned to adjust. But the nature of dementia is that it is a progressive disease, always changing. Just when I got used to a particular loss, a new one would crop up. Not only did I have to adjust to Harvey's changes, I had to learn how to operate in the world of managing the household and our medical clinic.

Once he passed away, I had to adapt to a new schedule and way of thinking about my day. I shifted from being a caregiver to a widow. Retirement a year later led to a loss of my identity as a physician. There was a move to a new house in the same time frame, and a daughter that married and another that graduated from college and moved out. So many life changes. I had to learn how to live by myself and fill my days. Hiking and travel became a priority, and while on the trails, if I paid attention, nature taught me how to adapt to change. Plant and animal adaptation and specialization especially fascinate me. It's as if the plants and animals think, *How can I best fit into my environment, attract the best mate, or spread my pollen most efficiently?* So they develop this perfect adaptation or that particular specialization in order to achieve these goals.

Two particular flowers with especially odd shapes made me want to know more. There are sixty to seventy species of columbine found throughout the Northern Hemisphere, and they can also be cultivated in gardens. What makes the blossoms peculiar looking are the long spurs that extend off the back of the petals. These spurs are filled with nectar that attract their pollinators—moths, butterflies, and hummingbirds. Moths and butterflies uncoil their long, tubelike proboscises into the flower's spur and siphon out the nectar. Hummingbirds use their tongues to lap up the sweet liquid. While they are drinking in the nectar, pollen attaches to the legs, wings, and bodies of the pollinators, who then fly away and distribute the pollen across their territories. What's amazing to me is the variety of spur shapes the columbine flower takes. The spurs may be long or short, straight or curved. Each species of columbine has adapted their spurs to fit the length and shape of their particular pollinator's tongue or beak. Likewise, each pollinator's tongue or beak has become adapted to fit a particular spur shape. It's mutually beneficial.

The mountain laurel flower has a unique method of distributing its pollen. The stamen, the parts of the flower that produce pollen, are not upright as they are in most flowers, but are tethered down into pockets within the petals of the cup-shaped blooms. When a pollinator, such as a bee, lands on the blossom, the weight of the bee causes the spring-loaded stamen to pop out of their pockets like catapults and shower the bee with pollen.

How did these flowers "think" of these ingenious ways to ensure their species? The answer is evolution. The plants whose pollen was more successfully distributed had a reproductive advantage.

Caregivers to loved ones living with a form of dementia can take a cue from nature and evolve their approach to caregiving. We even have the added benefit of being able to think and learn in real time, not in the millions of years it takes for the natural world to change. A first step is to mentally enter their world. If we can see the world from their point of view, a solution may present itself. Then if we try one approach, and it doesn't get the desired result, we can adapt and change the tactic. And keep shifting and trying new approaches. It's a necessity, too, because what worked well at one stage of the disease just might not work at all in the next.

Trying the same failed approach over and over just isn't ever going to work—whether in giving care or in living life as a human being. It's hard to break old habits and ways of thinking as our lives change, but we have to evolve with our changing reality over time. Life is never static, and what once worked might not always. It's imperative that we adapt to our current reality.

NATURE'S EDUCATORS

The Galápagos Islands' most famous visitor was Charles Darwin. He boarded the HMS *Beagle* as a naturalist in 1831, at the age of twenty-two, and circumnavigated the globe on a five-year journey. Along the way, he made notes about geology and collected plant and animal species. The Galápagos Islands were just one short stop on the expedition. Though the HMS *Beagle* sailed among the islands for five weeks, Darwin only set foot on four of them, spending three days on Floreana and two weeks on Santiago. However, what he observed and collected there would change the world of science, and the world at large, forever.

On the islands, Darwin collected several birds that we now call Darwin's finches. At the time, he thought that they were each so distinctly different that they had to be unrelated. It was only after he returned to England with these preserved birds that the ornithologist John Gould would conclude that Darwin had collected eighteen distinct species of finch.

Remarkably, the finches of the Galápagos have continued to adapt and evolve in the present, not just over millennia. Modern scientific research, led by the married couple Peter and Rosemary Grant, has shown just how quickly a species can react to its changing environment. A severe drought in 1973 killed most of the finches on Daphne Major, the island where the Grants' studies take place. By meticulously measuring the beak size of each surviving bird on the island, they demonstrated that the remaining finches had larger beaks, thus they were better equipped to crack open the available nuts and seeds. They thrived because of their beak size, and they passed that trait on to succeeding generations, creating a new species.

Once again, the lesson here is that change is inevitable for all of us. But, how we react to those changes is up to us. Digging in our heels and refusing to acknowledge that change has occurred is not healthy. Denial is a powerful weapon when we don't want to see or accept a new reality. But it cannot last.

There are expected changes—babies enter our lives, adult children leave home, health issues appear as we age, we retire from a long career. Even though we know the changes are coming, they force us to grapple with a new way of living. It is harder to adjust to unexpected changes. If something isn't on our radar, we don't have time to prepare ourselves. These changes can be shocking, and can knock us off our feet, throwing life out of balance.

Eventually, the healthy approach is to adapt to the changes. For example, we cannot ignore a badly sprained ankle, because walking on it is painful and will further injure it. By adjusting our gait, a limp might accommodate the sprain for a while, but placing a brace on the ankle for support and allowing the ankle to heal is a better adaptation.

Examination of the changes in our lives, both expected and unexpected, shows us where we need to make adjustments and accommodations. Maybe we even need some added outside support, like the ankle brace. Whatever the change, adapting to our current environment, like the finches in the Galápagos Islands, will ensure a better quality of life.

Miraculous, everyday transformations occur all over the animal kingdom. One day when our daughters were very young, I found a colorful caterpillar munching on a fennel plant that I had recently planted in our garden. Instead of getting angry at the very hungry caterpillar, I decided we would have a family science lesson. So I brought it into the house and created an environment for it in a mason jar, setting it on a shelf near our family's kitchen table. I planned to feed the caterpillar from the fennel plant, and we would just watch to see what happened. The caterpillar ate and ate the fresh fennel, getting fatter and fatter. Our girls were fascinated by the poop that it excreted and how it shed its skins while growing bigger.

One morning at breakfast, a few weeks after I brought it in, I noticed that the caterpillar was not moving at all, seemingly tethered at its head and feet. I wondered if it had died. A few minutes later, I noticed that it was twitching and moving, almost violently. I called the family to come see, and over a ten-minute period, we watched as our caterpillar gradually transformed into a chrysalis—squirming the whole time. We first noticed a patch of light green on the back of its head that then spread over the entire body, engulfing the caterpillar. A minute or two later, the process was complete, and the chrysalis was immobile.

I was surprised by this process. I wasn't sure, but I thought that maybe a caterpillar formed a shell, excreting it from their body somehow. I didn't realize that the caterpillar itself became a chrysalis. And I was surprised that it looked as if the bug were struggling against the transformation. I wanted to reassure it by saying, "It's OK, little caterpillar! I know you don't understand what's happening to you right now, but if you just relax and let this happen, you'll soon emerge as something wonderful and beautiful." I later learned that the squirming is a way for it to wriggle out of the last of its skins. The light green patch that appeared was the chrysalis breaking open the old skin that was eventually shed.

Two weeks later, again at breakfast, I noticed a crack in the now dull brown chrysalis, with a few spindly black legs emerging from it. Now our family watched as a crumpled wad of a brand-new butterfly emerged, clinging to the spent shell by its extravagantly long legs. Taking the jar outdoors, I gently shook it out onto the railing of our front porch, which was bathed in sunshine. As we continued to watch, this gorgeous creature slowly began to unfurl its wrinkled wings. It began to move them, pumping blood throughout the black- and blue-colored wings so that they stiffened and became rigid enough for flight. And fly our black swallowtail butterfly did. My heart soared as it took off. What a miracle it was, and a miracle that we got to witness such a transformation.

It's still a mystery *how* the chrysalis transforms into a butterfly. Scientists say that the creature inside turns to mush, a soup of proteins and genetic material, that then rearranges itself to create a butterfly. Sounds like a miracle to me.

Butterflies have long been a symbol of resurrection and rebirth—changing from one type of creature into another. But what most struck me after witnessing this firsthand was the struggle that the caterpillar seemed to put up as it became a chrysalis. It felt so relatable! When we know that we need to change, we often fight it, putting up our defenses, using the techniques our egos have successfully used in the past. If change is inevitable, though, we should learn to let go, give in to it, and let it happen.

I believe that we are called, in different times in our lives, to put ourselves into the loving arms of the Divine, to rest in protection, as the work of transformation takes place. Our former self gives way to a new self. It's hard to let go of the known and trust that transformation will be good for us, that we will emerge from it a new and more beautiful creature.

But it's never just a rest. It can be hard work to shed our old skin, ridding ourselves of tired and worn-out ways of being. While in the chrysalis, we may try to rearrange our old self to become a new self, but it requires trust and surrender to the chrysalis of Divine love. We don't know what we will emerge as, but when we do emerge, it's imperative that we bathe in the sunshine of the same Divine love so that we can soar.

Autumn is the time of year when monarch butterflies make their way south to overwinter in warmer climates. Here in Alabama, we are on that migration path, so we can witness monarchs on their journey southward in the fall season. Once, while staying at the Grand Hotel in Fair Hope, Alabama, I came across several monarchs. Evidently, they are a symbol of the Grand, as they stop here every year to lap up the nectar from flowering plants that are specifically planted for them. I was able to take several close-up photographs of these beauties. One even landed on my chest, directly over my heart, and rested there for several seconds.

I've learned about this migration through the years, with some facts that have truly surprised me. Scientists only relatively recently, in 1975, discovered the location of their overwintering site in central Mexico. Indigenous peoples have been aware of the mass of butterflies that form huge roosting colonies in the branches of oyamel fir trees, but US scientists were not. Prior to that "discovery," scientists thought that monarchs overwintered as pupae, or singly. I was astounded that we didn't know of this until so recently. I even pulled out my father's old *National Geographic* magazines and found an article from that time describing the discovery.

Another amazing fact about the migration is that scientists have been tracking the monarchs by placing identification tags on their wings, now as tiny stickers, the diameter of pencil erasers. Then, volunteers collect dead butterflies and mail them back to the laboratory.

A single monarch is not capable of making the journey, which can be up to thirty thousand miles round trip. It takes four generations of butterflies to complete the cycle, with the southbound monarchs living eight times as long as their parents and grandparents. Beginning in March, monarchs leave their roosts in Mexico to begin the journey north. Along the way, female butterflies lay their eggs only on the milkweed plant. The resultant caterpillars then chow down on the milkweed leaves until it's time to form a chrysalis. The emergent butterflies then continue the migration northward until it's time to stop, mate, and lay eggs. This process continues until the fall.

The migration southward begins in September or October, and the five hundred thousand or so monarchs arrive at the roosting site in November. They remain there during the winter months, then the cycle begins again in March. To make this long southbound journey, monarchs enter a phase termed *diapause*, putting a pause to reproduction so that all their energy resources can be used to accumulate and store lipids that will provide the nourishment needed to make the trek.

That monarch that landed on my heart had probably already traveled a great distance and was fueling up to continue on to central Mexico. I felt blessed by that butterfly just as I felt blessed when my family witnessed the swallowtail's transformation from caterpillar to butterfly.

It felt like a blessing for me on my life's journey. I want to believe that she was telling me, "You have come far, Renée. You have still farther to go. Rest up, fuel up, get a sense of where you're next going. Home in on home, where you will be surrounded with warmth and comfort. But enjoy this journey too. It's fascinating!"

Another animal associated with transformation and change is the snake. Snakes strike fear in many people. It's one of those pervasive fears, like the fear of spiders, that I somehow don't subscribe to. I'm not sure why, but neither of these creatures cause me too much alarm, though I have a good healthy respect for snakes.

There are venomous varieties where I live, and once, I saw one stretched out on a trail while I was on a hike. It was a small rattlesnake, about twelve inches long, with a striking gray-and-black pattern and a very small rattle. I didn't study the snake for very long, and I should have taken a photo to verify what species it was, but later research led me to conclude it was a pygmy rattlesnake. While the snake tasted the air with its forked tongue, my hiking companion and I stepped gingerly around it from behind.

When my daughter and her friends visited the lake house one late August, they found a flattened snakeskin in the outdoor closet that stores all our water sports equipment. The skin was underneath our rolled-up lily pad, the giant floating raft we use to laze on the lake. I speculated that the snake got into the closet, shed its skin, then someone deposited the lily pad onto the unseen, freshly shed skin and flattened it. It was really quite fascinating, and we left the skin where we found it.

Unlike the butterfly, who transforms into a whole new creature when it sheds its chrysalis, the snake, and other creatures that shed, just outgrows its skin. During cicada season in Alabama, I find their shells almost daily, clinging to the trunk of a tree, a downspout, or even my outdoor stairs.

Shedding one's skin in order to begin anew has long been a metaphor for starting over. There is something poetic, beautiful, and a little sad about outgrowing oneself. I sometimes wish I could physically shed my ill-fitting old self as I grow into a new phase of my life or realize a new truth when the old one no longer serves me. It would be satisfying to have such a literal sign of new growth.

Personal growth occurs when we realize that we can't continue in our same worn patterns, and we move forward. If we can't let go of something that keeps us from growing, our spirit dies. We cannot cling to old thought patterns when we have stretched beyond them. And no one can force us to hold on to our old skins; we must shed them of our own accord.

We can do this metaphorically when we feel that we have outgrown old habits, thoughts, or ways of seeing the world. Maybe we write down that way of thinking onto a piece of paper and burn it. Maybe it's as simple as saying a prayer for the person we used to be and wishing them well. We can create meaningful rituals that mark a passage from one chapter of life into the next. Even if we don't recognize growth and shedding when it's happening, we can look back with compassion at the persons we were and appreciate that the skin that used to serve us has now fallen away to reveal something new.

THE ONLY CONSTANT IS CHANGE

Visual and physical reminders about change can be found in other areas of life and nature too. One summer, I received some unwanted, but necessary, news about the property at my lake house: The seawall was being undermined. When a flagstone on top of the wall sank into a hole, I called the company that installed it twelve years earlier. The contractor who came out remembered the project and told me that his crew still talked about the massive undertaking that it was. Evidently, because of the steep grade of the land, accessibility to the seawall is nearly nonexistent. He told me that everything—every bucket of gravel, every large stone—had to be transported by hand. They had installed new stone stairs to improve accessibility, and even increased lawn space for better staging. This was all news to me. In fact, the main reason I fell in love with the property was the isolation afforded by the steep embankment and the multilayered stone walls. It was an artful job.

However, because the crew from twelve years ago was unable to transport the preferred massive-sized boulders to create the seawall, they used smaller rocks, then backfilled it with gravel and dirt, and used cement to seal the areas between the rocks. Now, because of boat-wake waves lapping onto the wall, that backfill was being sucked out and washed away.

Water is powerfully destructive. Ask any victim of flooding. Or someone who has been caught in a riptide. Or involved in a surfing or boating accident. Even a belly flop into a placid pool can hurt like hell.

But I have seen the result of beautiful destruction, when flowing water creates canyons of all sizes over eons of years. The Grand Canyon is one majestic example, but smaller slot canyons offer a different perspective. On an alpine hiking trip in Switzerland, I witnessed how precisely water carves stone. Just thirty minutes into our first walk, we entered the Aare

Gorge. As we followed a trail of cantilevered paths alongside one of two opposing towering cliffs, the power of water was immediately evident. Below was the turquoise-colored rushing river of glacial melt, and on either side, the walls of the canyon twisted, worn smooth into sinuous curves. The last day of our trek led us through another gorge, Orridi di Uriezzo, in Italy. This one was narrower and had no water running through it. Walking through this chasm of rock walls, worn into voluptuous curves, was another reminder of the power of moving water.

And like the sensuous curves in the two gorges, I, too, can sometimes experience transformation through destructive power. I am strong like stone, but weak enough to be worn and changed into something beautiful. Life's trials have polished some of my rough edges, removing layers of my ego-armor, and creating something new and more alive in its smoother surface. I don't curse the power of water or the power of life's challenges. They make me who I am. Changed. Softened. New.

Yet another type of remarkable adaptation can be found in trees. I came across an interesting tree while hiking in Oak Mountain State Park, our nearest state park. It had a trunk that appeared normal enough at earth level, but then it seemed to spread out and merge with a large rock near its base. Above the rock, it looked like a normal tree again. I've seen saplings bent at odd angles as they grew around an obstacle, but I've never seen a mature tree so fully adapted around a boulder. I imagine the sapling grew near the base of this boulder, then probably continued to reach for the sun by growing out and away from the rock. As it started to push upward again, it continued to encounter the obstacle, but molded itself to the contour of the boulder, trying always to grow upward. Once it had grown beyond the outcrop of rock, it could resume its vertical climb toward the sun, now unhindered.

I was certainly changed by Harvey's disease. It molded me

into a new creature as I adapted and shifted and adjusted to my new life. Now that part of my life is over, and I have continued on, though I am left with scars from that time that will never go away. I didn't have the wherewithal to know what I was doing, bending and reshaping my life to fit the circumstances at the time. I just did what needed to be done. And it changed me.

I was a strong person before Harvey's diagnosis, but I really came into my strength during that time. I learned to assess situations rapidly and make challenging decisions. In the past, I sometimes dithered with some decisions, but now, I just make them. Why put off a decision when I can take care of it now?

Prior to our family's time with Alzheimer's disease, I had a fairly balanced work-home lifestyle. During Harvey's illness, the balance was harder to achieve just because of all the additional tasks required of me. I learned that taking care of myself didn't necessarily mean spa retreats or shopping. It became more about what brought me peace and joy—nature, artistic endeavors, reading, writing, and deep friendships.

When I became a widow, my role as a caregiver ended. Because I had never stopped working as a primary care physician, I didn't find the loss of the caregiver role as difficult as many others experience. In fact, it was a relief not to carry that burden any longer. And I felt guilty about feeling relieved. By then, too, I had shouldered all the responsibilities of running the clinic and the household, so those roles didn't change. But without Harvey, I was at loose ends at times, trying to figure out how to spend my now expanded free time. I managed to fill it with friendships, time with our daughters, and the outdoors.

And when I retired, I gave up the role of physician. It took about nine months to come to that decision, contemplating different scenarios I could place myself in—part-time clinical work or various administrative roles. In the end, I decided I really just didn't want to work anymore, nor did I need to—for financial or personal reasons. I decided not to even renew my license, as it would be quite expensive, and I reasoned that I could take the steps to reactivate it in the future if I desired. My next step was to lean into the role of retired person—walking, hiking, and traveling. I was free of the duties that bound me to all but myself, and that freedom allowed me time to explore what truly moved me and motivated me.

After retirement, I wrote my memoir and began speaking to caregivers at conferences, seminars, and even one-on-one when called upon. This was my new calling. I keep thinking this phase of my life will end, but new people are diagnosed with dementia daily. The need for understanding and support will always be there. As long as I am asked to speak, I will. As long as I feel I have something useful to say, I will write.

I value my own life much more now, trying not to take it for granted. I want to live and be healthy for much longer. I want to enjoy time with my family doing the active things we like to do together. So I am taking better care of my health.

But I carry deep, tender wounds from those years of Harvey's time with Alzheimer's disease too. Scarring is taking place, so that the wounds are not quite as raw now, but like that tree, the scars are there; they have molded me into the person I am today. I am marked, but I will continue to grow and reach for the sun, transforming and adapting myself as my circumstances call for it. There will always be a need to mold myself to fit whatever life's journey has for me.

CHAPTER 8

I Already Have All That I Need

Opening my eyes and my heart to what's just beyond my own back door has led me to adventures and aha moments that I never knew I needed. I learned this even more clearly after purchasing a rustic lake house on Lay Lake in central Alabama. It is located just north of Lay Dam and is part of the Coosa River system. An old map I found shows that there was once a fish camp on the property. The house was built in stages, so perhaps the old fish camp is part of my house even now. Sited on a slope down to the lake, the house has three floors for indoor living and three separate outdoor levels—a layer cake of vistas.

What sold me on this property was the view from the back porches and the dock. It doesn't directly face the lake; rather, there is an island that separates my property from the open water, with a narrow but deep channel between my shore and the island. It gives me the feeling of privacy, and, as I soon discovered, is home to abundant wildlife. Though I've only had this lake house for a short time, already I've witnessed and encountered many wild creatures, some in their world, some in mine.

Sitting on one of the back porches of the lake house, I can watch great egrets, cormorants, ducks, hummingbirds, Canada geese, turkey vultures, and a solitary great blue heron. I've even seen two bald eagles riding a thermal high above the treetops, and I once witnessed an osprey drop a fish it was carrying and then dive back down to the lake's surface to retrieve it.

On my very first day at the lake house, I saw two hummingbirds flitting around the deck, dive-bombing each other. I've never seen these tiny birds at my primary home, despite my attempts at luring them with various feeders. So I brought my unused hummingbird feeder on my next visit to the lake, filled it, and hung it eight feet away from my favorite reading and writing spot. Not ten minutes later, I had a visitor. It buzzed around a bit, took a quick sip of the nectar, then buzzed off. A few minutes later, it returned, perched, and drank for a solid two minutes. From my vantage point, I could even watch its minute tongue lap up the sweet fluid.

Cormorants are aquatic birds that dive under the water for fish, popping up several feet from where they initially dove. When they paddle on the surface of the water, their bodies are mostly submerged because their feathers become waterlogged from diving. To dry off, they stand on a sunny rock or treetop with their wings half spread, looking like bedraggled black rag dolls. There is a flock of them on the island, and they all silently swoop out together in the morning. They gather again in the branches of the pine trees in the evenings, now decidedly not silent. The first time I heard them making their strange noises, I thought a herd of wild boar were on the island. But no, cormorants neither sing nor squawk; they grunt like pigs when settling in with the flock.

I love watching the great blue heron stalk and hunt its prey in the shallows, moving like a tai chi master in the grasses.

And watching it fly off lightens my heart as it performs a port de bras of elegantly slow, undulating wingbeats. But when the bird opens its beak, it is pure pterodactyl roar.

One lazy, quiet early September afternoon at the lake, I heard a chittering as a bird skimmed across the surface of the lake. I knew that sound—a belted kingfisher. I watched as it perched on an exposed branch of a tree on the island across from my lake house. It first scanned the water, then plunged headlong into the lake to retrieve a small fish. It also made several runs alone, and later with its mate, down the channel that separates my shore from the island's shore.

In my kayak one fall afternoon, I noticed a few animals swimming in the water directly in front of me. I assumed they were the ubiquitous cormorants and that they would fly off. But as I drew nearer, I could see that it was a family of three raccoons swimming to my island. Their little heads were bobbing above the water, making good time. It might not be its official name, but that island is now Raccoon Island in my mind.

There are turtles who swim near my dock and bask in the sun on half-submerged logs. When I get into my kayak to paddle around Raccoon Island, I can get especially close to them if I manage to dip my paddle silently. The egrets and the great blue heron sometimes squawk and fly away as I slip into the shallow areas with them to examine the plants and trees more closely.

As I watch and live with these creatures, I have learned from them. These animals have everything they need right there at the lake—food, shelter, companionship—things I have, but frequently take for granted. They also have internal instincts that tell them all they need to know. Maybe I need to lean into the notion that I already have all the internal wisdom I need to make my way forward. If I live my life as if all my longings and desires can be found by digging deep into what I already know—from my lived experiences, from my intuition—then I am more than halfway on the journey to my true self.

So I've learned to drink deeply of that which truly nourishes me. Or to gather noisily with my flock of friends and family, with a bit of good-natured banter. Or alone, to dance a silent ballet or else to fearlessly defend my place. Or to put down my technology and rely on my instincts for rising, eating, and resting. Or to relax in the sun, rolling into the cool water when the time feels right to swim to a different shore.

WHAT IS HOME?

The iconic animal of the Galápagos Islands is the Galápagos giant tortoise. My father and I, along with all the other passengers aboard our ship, had the opportunity to learn more about these animals and to stroll among them. Tortoise day took place on Santa Cruz Island, where we learned that there were once fifteen subspecies of the Galápagos tortoise. Only thirteen have survived the many years of human exploitation and habitat destruction, and they now live on seven different islands.

These monster-sized tortoises have no natural predators, so they have evolved to live for an exceedingly long time, continuing to grow during their entire lives. They can weigh close to nine hundred pounds, and one captive female lived to be 175 years old.

The differences among some of the subspecies provided Darwin with clues that led to his theory of evolution. Tortoises in the lush green highlands have shorter necks and domed shells, and graze on grass and low-growing shrubs. The subspecies who live in the lower dry areas are called *saddlebacks* and have a large notch in their shell, through which they can extend their long necks. Like the Galápagos finches, the different subspecies of tortoises have adapted to their particular environments. Those living in more humid locations nibble at ground level while the species living in drier climates eat cacti in the area, stretching their necks up to nab the fruit. The cacti, in turn evolving alongside the saddleback tortoise, have trunks like trees as a defense against the hungry tortoises.

That's all very interesting, but to actually walk among them was amazing. Donning galoshes to prevent ant bites, we walked among scattered individual tortoises, of all different ages and sizes, chomping away on grass. They paid us no attention, not even pulling in their heads when we came close. And I realized that some of these guys were older than my eighty-eight-year-old father.

The tortoise's shell is an adaptive rib cage. You can see that evidence on the inside of a shell. The shell is also its home, and as such, is part of its being. The tortoise doesn't dig a burrow or a nest for itself. It doesn't find a den or build a house. All its sheltering needs are provided by its own body.

What if we take our cue from the tortoise and realize that all we need is already a part of us? The good life we seek, the treasure we hunt, is intrinsically within. We don't need to look outside of ourselves. The answer can be found if we go into our interior to discover it. This is a lovely metaphor, but we humans don't have shells to call home like tortoises. We need to seek housing for shelter.

I began to wonder about the concept of *home* while on my Galápagos trip. I had moved into my little gem of a house six years prior, downsizing from our large family home. I decided to move when Harvey became a permanent resident in a memory care facility and our daughters had grown and were living on their own. Knowing the family home would sell quickly, I bought my new house before I sold the old one. And because the new house was about half the size of the old one, I decided which furniture and decor would fit and that I loved most, then took that with me and sold the rest.

I had been lonely rambling around that big house full of memories, and I didn't have much to do to occupy my expanded free time, now that caregiving took up so much less of it. I might have needed a constructive project to distract me, to insulate and protect my heart. I don't think I intentionally ran away from our family home, but rather, it seemed like a new start, a new place for my new life. But how was this new house going to feel like home without those I most loved to populate it? If "home is where the heart is," and my heart was scattered, how would this new house ever feel right?

Despite my concerns, my small cottage soon felt like home to me, partly because I was surrounded by my favorite things that reminded me of my favorite people. More importantly, I came to realize that my heart is ultimately my own, and I will be home no matter where I choose to live. Home is not a place.

Seven years after downsizing, and six years after Harvey passed away, I began yearning for a new house. I loved my cute cottage that felt like a tree house, but a few problems loomed. There was the flight of concrete stairs to the front door. I really didn't mind the stairs, which situated the house high above the street, nestled in the trees. But my guests did, especially my octogenarian parents. Then my parked car was sideswiped by a hit-and-run driver because there is only off-street parking, and that became the last straw. I decided it was time to look for another house.

While I was on a trip to Ithaca, Greece, with twenty fellow travelers, my real estate agent (who is also my beloved sister, Andrea) alerted me to a house that fit all the criteria and seemed perfect. Because I was far across the Atlantic Ocean, Andrea and one of my daughters FaceTimed with me as they toured the house. With their blessing and encouragement, I put in an offer on it. However, I was outbid, so that one got away.

I remained somewhat ambivalent about this new-house idea. I loved my little cottage, and because I wasn't that upset about losing out on the house that I had toured virtually, what was I really looking for? What was really behind this desire to move?

On Ithaca, our group was immersed in the story of Odysseus—his hero's journey and return home to the island—and we were reflecting on the theme of *home*. What does *home* mean? Is it a place from our past or our family's past? Is it a feeling? Is it nostalgia?

That's when I realized what I really wanted: a house that was a bit larger. In the cottage, I could not entertain larger gatherings. A quaint home is not conducive to Thanksgiving dinners or even larger parties. Not that I am a big entertainer, but I wanted to be able to host my extended family of about twenty, at least occasionally.

I realized that I wanted more people in my life. The time of isolation and insulation had passed. After seven years in the bungalow, my heart had mostly recovered. It'd grown, too, and I wanted to expand my hearth to match the expansion of my heart.

As part of my preparation for the pilgrimage to Greece, I reread Homer's *Iliad* and *Odyssey*, the classic tales of the hero's journey. Odysseus sets out from his home on the island of Ithaca to fight in the Trojan War. He leaves behind his wife, Penelope, and their infant son, Telemachus. The war lasts ten years, and it takes him another ten years to make it back home. Those last ten years are the stories that make up *Odyssey*, a series of adventures and encounters with monsters and sorceresses. When he finally does make it back to Ithaca, he finds his home has been besieged by scores of suitors, young men vying for Penelope's hand, as it is presumed that Odysseus has died. Once the suitors are taken care of, Odysseus is truly "home."

This archetypal story has endured the centuries because it is all our stories. In literature, there are three main parts of the hero's journey. First, the decision to leave, whether by choice or circumstance. There may be a call to leave, or there may be a flight. The hero may prepare for the journey by gathering information, using a map, or relying on a wise instructor or mentor. Next, the journey itself with all the hardships and joys encountered by the hero. The last section is the homecoming, when the hero returns, recounting all they have learned and using their personal reincarnation to inform and transform their community.

We are each the heroes in our individual journeys, answering the call and finding our way while encountering danger, temptation, and serendipity. We grapple with pain, sorrow, and other monsters in our lives. We learn to live as human beings in this world. And if our journey is successful, we will return home wiser, rejuvenated, restored, and ready to bring that hard-won wisdom to the community. Odysseus journeyed out of the chaos of war and eventually made it back home. Out of the chaos of our lives, if we pay attention to what we have encountered along the way, we can make the same trip back home, home to our true selves.

I believe that we were born as pure sparks of divinity. Just look into the eyes of a young child. There is no guile, no deceit, no cunning. It's the idea of original blessing, not original sin, that resonates with me. As we mature and grow, we become more and more acquainted with the world. As a defense to what we encounter, we develop an ego that protects our tender original spark, a shield that prevents the storms of life from snuffing out that spark. Our adult ego leads us around until it no longer works for us. The lies that our egos tell us—"you're not good enough," "you are not special," "you don't matter"—begin to cause the spark within to dim. When we realize this truth during our individual hero's journey, either from a critical mass of suffering or through inner work, we become more conscious that this way of living doesn't work. We wake up to the reality of our true selves, the original blessed child of light. This is the spiritual journey, the reflection of Odysseus's tale.

All hero's journey stories teach us this lesson. The way back to ourselves, the way home, the way back to who we were created to be—not who we created our egos to be—is the journey we are each called to make.

While on the island of Ithaca, we had the chance to visit the ruins of the possible site of Odysseus and Penelope's palace. In Homer's tale, Penelope and her infant son stay home for the ten years that Odysseus is away fighting the Trojan War and for the following ten years that it takes him to return home. During that time, Penelope not only runs her household and raises their son, but she also uses her wits to hold off the suitors camping out at the palace. She claims she will choose one of them when she completes the burial shroud of her father-in-law. In fact, she weaves all day but unravels the cloth at night. When Odysseus finally returns home, Penelope doesn't initially recognize him, but eventually she welcomes him when he accurately describes their marriage bed.

If the metaphor of the hero's journey is overcoming life's challenges in order to come home to our true selves, what is the heroine's journey? Is Penelope a heroine in this particular part of the story? Do we even need heroine stories? Shouldn't the hero's journey cover all genders if it is really a metaphor for the discovery of the self? The hero and heroine may come to the same discovery of self, but how they achieve it in classical Western thought is very different.

The male hero sets out from home and is tested in strength, cunning, and daring. He must prove his worth and mettle as a man within these realms. Greek mythology and legends abound with hero stories that follow this trajectory, and their adventures are specifically masculine and testosterone laden.

We all have to face trials in life. We are all called to make the journey to ourselves. But in these stories, women are not expected to physically fight or even to leave home. The heroine's journey, as personified by Penelope, was not a journey, but a staying put, waiting for the return of her husband. Penelope's discovery of her true self happens while she stays in one location, her home. She moves forward in her personal growth as she uses her wits to stall the suitors and wait for Odysseus. The moment of homecoming is when she recognizes Odysseus as her "home."

On another of our days in Greece, our group ventured to the ruins of Eleusis. The Eleusinian Mysteries were secret reenactments and rituals of the myth of Demeter and Persephone that, during ancient times, drew people from all over the known world. The mysteries that were imparted to the pilgrims were so rigorously guarded that very few details about the rites are available to us today, though we do still have the story they are based on.

Demeter, sister of Zeus, was the goddess of the harvest, and is often depicted with her daughter, Persephone. As the story goes, when Demeter walked upon the earth, planting grain for humanity and tending the fruit trees and fields, Persephone danced alongside her. One day, Hades, another of Zeus's siblings and god of the underworld, decided he wanted Persephone as his bride, so he opened a hole in the earth, and she was swallowed into his dark world. Persephone was very sad in this cold, silent, and lonely world, and Demeter was distraught at the loss of her beloved daughter. Because of Demeter's grief, the land stopped producing and became barren. Zeus intervened at Demeter's behest and demanded that Hades release Persephone. Demeter and Persephone were reunited with overwhelming joy, but because she had eaten the fruit of the dead while in the underworld, Persephone would have to return every year. When mother and daughter are together during the spring and summer, the world is fruitful and plentiful, but when Persephone returns to Hades, the fallowness of winter overtakes the land.

Judging from the scant written record, traveling to Eleusis and partaking of the rites and rituals was evidently a life-altering and life-affirming experience. The timeless theme of death and rebirth into a new life that was reenacted gave the pilgrims renewed hope, just as these themes do for us today. All civilizations have had, and still have, these resurrection themes; it's not exclusive to the Christian worldview. It's astounding how similar these myths and mysteries are across time and place, and how much hope they bring to us. We can be reborn into a new self. The caterpillar morphs into the butterfly. The snake sheds its skin. The circle continues. The Earth turns on her axis. The seasons spiral onward. Winter gives way to spring.

The myth of Demeter and Persephone is a remnant of the more ancient goddess worship. As warrior civilizations overpowered agrarian ones, earth goddesses were supplanted by the pantheons of powerful male gods and their less important sibling and consort goddesses. Demeter was probably a demoted Mother Earth goddess, but she still held an important role in the lives of the people in classical Greece. In ancient times, worship of the earth goddess as bringer of life into the world was prevalent. Not only did the goddess bring forth vegetative life from the earth, but she ushered in human life as well. Childbirth was a revered, but dangerous, endeavor in the ancient world. The heroine's journey of birthing children came with a great price, so it was seen as heroic and holy.

Maybe modern men and women can draw on both the hero and the heroine's myths—Odysseus and Penelope, Demeter and Persephone, as well as that of the ancient earth goddesses. This is the journey of self-discovery—as we venture out into the world, or as we nurture our homes, or as we celebrate our roles of being the bringers and the co-creators of life.

THE ANSWER IS INSIDE

Our group of travelers to Greece also traveled to Delphi, where ruins of a temple are still imbued with a sense of awe and holiness. Within the temple, the Oracle, usually an older woman, would supply an answer to a question brought by a pilgrim who had made the journey there. As our group approached, we were invited, if we wanted, to bring a question of our own to the place within the temple where the Oracle would have sat. Then one by one, as the rest of us held space for each individual, we stepped to the entrance of the temple, and in varying forms of prayer, silently asked our question, then waited for a response. Some stood with arms upraised. Others knelt. One prostrated himself directly on the ramp leading into the temple.

I was led to sway back and forth, shifting my weight rapidly from one foot to the other in a dance of sorts, chanting to myself in time with my movement, "Should I? Should I? Should I . . . ?" I then gradually lifted my arms as I asked my question. When I knew it was time to stop my dance to listen for the answer, I dropped my arms and held my palms upward to receive.

My question was "Should I actively pursue dating?" The response came back: "You will know when the time is right." Just as ambiguous as most responses pilgrims from ancient times received from the Oracle. But I wasn't surprised. Most often, I *do* know. Eventually. My inner knowing is usually right, if I take the time to stop and listen to it. The answer is within me. Everything I need is already there. And I suspect that's what the Oracle of Delphi imparted to pilgrims long ago as well with her roundabout responses, leading the individual to puzzle it out on their own.

The very act of bringing a question to Delphi was deliberate for each of us in the group. I could have asked myself or trusted sources my question right from my home. But making a planned journey to this site gifted me with a presence I wouldn't have normally had. Because I had the focus and intention and expectation, I could ask and then receive the answer in a quiet knowing, acknowledging my own sense of trusting in myself to find the answer.

When you think about what's inside yourself, you might start with the literal: The structure of our human body is the skeleton. Made up of 206 individual bones, the skeleton provides support and protection for our bodies just as the tortoise's shell provides structure for theirs.

I learned a technique that taps into this intrinsic scaffolding that anchors our muscles while on my alpine trekking trip in Switzerland. Called the mountaineer's rest step, it relies on the strength of the skeleton to bear the weight of one's body instead of relying solely on the musculature. To do this, the climber must maintain a good, upright posture—no slumping allowed. When stepping up, the downhill leg should be straight, locked in place, and the uphill foot provides balance but does not bear much weight. The straight line of the skeleton, from skull through spine and down to the downhill leg, is the framework holding it all in place while engaging fewer muscle fibers. Waiting a microsecond in the position resets the body. The next step transfers the hiker's weight from the previous downhill foot as it becomes the uphill one to the new downhill leg, which now locks into a straight position. Those microseconds of rest with each step add up to provide more energy for a long, arduous ascent.

Our built-in skeletal structure is like our internal strength. When we rely on our known strengths—integrity, honesty, and resilience, for example—we don't have to overuse or overthink peripheral constructs. Our scaffolding of inner strength will carry us forward. Otherwise, we may try to power through with a force of will, or concentrate our interior resources in obsessing about choices, going around in circles, or dithering. Taking the next right step is easier when we rely on those qualities of soul structure.

Going forward in my life as a single person would have felt very daunting just ten years ago, but because of all the years of running the household and the medical office by myself, I knew that I had the knowledge and wisdom to go it alone. When I was married, I would have asked Harvey's opinion about even minor concerns about the budget, the children's school, or issues at the clinic. But now I have developed a clear-eyed strength and resilience to make good decisions on my own. I have learned to trust my inner knowing.

***

The hero's journey is a metaphor for our lives—venturing out into the world (or staying put), encountering life's hurdles and overcoming them, and then returning home with new wisdom that can be shared. It is all our stories. But we don't make just one journey. Even as we travel home to a closer version of our true selves, there will always be another journey, another lesson to learn.

And *home* can mean many things. It's a place, a feeling, a destination. Coming home to a truer version of who we were created to be is life's journey. The journey is meant to bring us closer to the god-spark that dwells within.

The animals at my lake house don't embark on a hero's journey. They have all that they need to have. They know all that they need to know. They are always living into their true selves. What a blessing that we humans have the gift of moving forward and changing and learning. As we journey closer to our true selves, our sense of inner knowing grows. I believe that truer self has a deep understanding that we can trust. It is our guide.

CHAPTER 9

The Freedom to Live

Mount Kilimanjaro was, physically, the most challenging hike I have accomplished, but a distant second was a twenty-mile hike at Oak Mountain State Park.

There were twenty-seven of us when we started. It was fifty degrees at 7:00 a.m. on a Saturday in December when we hit the trail. We ranged in age from eleven to eighty years old, and only three of us were female. All but I had a connection to the Boy Scouts of America. I had been invited to join this annual twenty-mile hike for several years by a friend of mine from church, the organizer of the hike, but I always scoffed at the idea. No way would I want to join a bunch of Boy Scouts in mid-December for a grueling slog. It sounded like some sort of misery that I wanted no part of. But when the organizer asked me again this particular year, I thought, *I wonder if I can do it. I think that I can.* There wasn't any commitment. I could bow out at the last minute if the weather was horrible or if my body didn't seem cooperative. So I said yes.

At sunrise, a handful of Boy Scouts, their leaders and parents, and friends and family of the organizer set off. I had never hiked with this many people before. Evidently, when you have this many people to corral, and some of them are preadolescent and adolescent boys, a certain type of leadership is required. I have never been barked at before, but we were given our marching orders in a tone that was military-like. To be honest, it rankled.

I have always been a fast walker, and I have to remind myself to slow down and take breaks. In previous group hikes, I have always been in the pack up front. Not this day. These guys set out at what felt like a trot. We were on a rigid schedule because we needed to complete the hike by sunset, a ten-hour time frame. The organizer had led this hike for twenty-five years, and he knew what pace we needed to set and how long our breaks should be. Not that I trailed or lagged behind, but I wasn't up front. I got to experience what it is like to be toward the rear. The front group would stop for a break, waiting for the rest of us to catch up, then would take off again as soon as we, the slower hikers, arrived, barely giving us time to catch our breath. It seemed so unfair. But I had been on the other side of that equation and knew how frustrating it can be to wait for a group. And we had to keep to the schedule.

We hiked seven miles, taking a couple of two-minute breaks along the way, then stopped for fifteen minutes to eat, use the restroom, and peel off unneeded layers of clothing. Then there were another seven miles, with another fifteen-minute lunch break before the last six miles back to our cars. In total, we hiked twenty miles in ten hours with a total elevation gain of four thousand feet. That means there was also a total elevation loss of four thousand feet, because it was one giant loop. And that's where my body felt it. I had blisters on the bottoms of my pinky toes and a bruise under a toenail from bumping up against my boot. And my knees, especially the right, were definitely feeling it. We ended the hike with a steep downhill. Easy on the lungs, but hell on the knees. Thank heaven for trekking poles. And ibuprofen.

We might have started with twenty-seven participants, but only fifteen of us completed it. I almost bailed out at mile fourteen, but decided to carry on, just for the challenge. I am proud of myself for sticking with it and completing the entire hike. I proved to myself that my body, mind, and spirit could do it.

Though I chose this particular challenge, we can't always choose those that come our way. Perhaps intentionally placing ourselves in situations that require more of us than we are comfortable with gives us the opportunity to see what we are capable of, so that when unexpected challenges do arise, we can more confidently face them. If we choose the path of least resistance all the time, we may never know how strong we are. Challenging ourselves can build our confidence, can make us feel more in control of our lives, and can provide us with opportunities to be positive examples for others.

COMING BACK TO LIFE

I didn't always have the strength to keep moving forward, meeting challenges head-on. Sometimes, I just wanted to curl up, pull the blanket over my head, and retreat into my private cave of depression. Only by journeying forth and encountering beauty in nature and community could I take the next step forward.

Even though I have spent my whole life residing in the South, it was only a few years ago that I first heard of the resurrection fern. I'm certain that I saw them growing on live oaks when I lived in Charleston, appreciating the abundant flowing fronds nestled on the branches. But I didn't know their name or their secret superpower until I'd moved into my new home.

Soon after I downsized into the new house, I noticed two small green ferns growing on the base of two of my Japanese magnolias. They were sweet and delicate, but I didn't realize exactly what they were. Some days later, they were dead. *Oh, well,* I thought. *I'm glad I noticed them before they died.* Then I promptly forgot about them. One day after a rain, the ferns were back. I remember thinking that this was odd, and decided to keep an eye on them, still not knowing what they were. Sure enough, when we didn't have rain for a few days, they turned brown and shriveled, then returned to their verdant selves after a rain. I started noticing more of them on old trees in my neighborhood and on boulders while on hikes in the forest. And sure enough, they cycled the same as mine did through drought and rain.

It wasn't until my friend Sonja, a professional photographer, wrote a short piece about a photograph she had taken that I learned the name of this plant. Her project involved shooting pictures of trees that had been used as sites of racial violence. When she searched for a particular tree in Harpersville, Alabama, she learned that it had died and fallen but had not yet been removed. When she found the fallen tree, she took photos of the resurrection ferns that were donning it. What a powerful contrast—resurrection amid a place with a past of unspeakable pain and brutality.

The resurrection fern is a true fern, but it is an epiphyte—that is, a plant that derives all its nutrients from the air. It has roots, but they function only to anchor the plant to its host, not to pull nutrients from the soil. It's neither parasitic nor mutualistic.

What I had witnessed with the ferns on my trees wasn't death. Instead, they had curled inward, exposing their undersides during drought conditions. But when it rains, a system of pores on the undersurface, which is now the exposed surface, collects the water and then channels it out to the rest of the plant, unfurling the fronds and returning it to lushness. The resurrection fern can lose up to 95 percent of its water content and survive—a superpower when considering that most plants can only lose 10 percent of their water before they succumb. It is estimated that the resurrection fern can live up to one hundred years in their desiccated state.

What if we, in times of personal or spiritual drought, turned inward and exposed our vulnerability? I know that I have had times when I felt shriveled and dead inside, all my resources having run dry. The burdens of providing care can do that to us, just as the burdens of many different life circumstances can. By curling in on ourselves, we may be protecting our tender places, but the shell that we erect can't let in the spiritual nourishment that we need.

Sometimes it is only by making our wounds visible, by being honest and vulnerable with ourselves and with our community, that we can allow ourselves to be resurrected. Then, when the reviving waters do return—and they always do if we are patient—we can open ourselves up and drink it in as we learn to live again.

I find that I am slowly coming back to life following the years of caregiving and grief. But this new life of almost complete freedom is not one I've had experience with. In the past, I was on a very prescribed path—high school, college, medical school, residency, physicianhood, and parenthood. Not that I felt trapped on this path. It's what I wanted, and my life was very rewarding.

Then my life's trail suddenly did a loop-de-loop, a hairpin turn that I didn't see coming, and I got vertigo and whiplash from the sudden change in direction. The trajectory I thought that I was on veered, and it was nothing that I could have foreseen.

So I tried to map a new path into this dark forest. I wasn't sure where I was going, and there wasn't much in the way of trail markers to point me in the right direction. I did the best that I could by researching, talking to people who had been on a similar path, and learning to just follow it wherever it led me.

I didn't ask for help so much as I learned to accept it. This made the trail a little less bumpy, smoothing the way. If I felt like I was floundering, stuck at a fork in the trail, not knowing which way to go, I often turned to trusted friends and family for advice. At times, a friend could see that I was headed in a wrong direction. Certain caregiving techniques no longer worked or I was doing something that had an untoward effect on me or my family. The friend would call me out of the woods and back onto the path.

Since Harvey's death and my retirement, I seem to be free of any prescribed, straightforward track. I followed a well-laid-out plan for publishing my memoir and marketing it, but the speaking engagements happen randomly, and I'm often left wondering, *Now what?*

I was contemplating this question while on my friend's pier at her home on Lake Martin after completing a particularly narrow, twisting hike. She has a wide-open view of the lake; the far shore is far indeed. I told her, "Maybe I'm not having to choose a certain path to take at this point. The whole expanse is ahead of me. I can choose to go anywhere!" (Figuratively, but maybe literally too.)

MAKING MEANING

After Harvey passed away, I wondered if I would ever dream about him. I'm not particularly sentimental, but I missed him terribly and longed to at least feel his presence once again. I remembered that my grandmother had hoped for such an experience after my grandfather passed away, and she was always disappointed that it never happened for her.

About two months after he died, I did indeed dream of Harvey. In the dream, he was his very ill self from the weeks leading up to his death. He was lying on his side in his hospital bed, in the beige-walled memory care unit, the rails of the bed up. The institutional blue cotton blanket covered most of his body, and the plush snowflake-patterned throw that I had given him for Christmas lay over his feet. His eyes were open, but they were blank and unseeing. He wasn't wearing his glasses, and for some reason, that particularly unmoored me. His hair was mussed and in dire need of a haircut, a three-day beard was sprouting, and his stale body odor mingled with the antiseptic smells of the nursing home.

I leaned over the railing of the bed from behind him and bent to kiss his cheek. I whispered, "How are you doing today, Harvey?" In the dream, even though he hadn't spoken meaningful words for months, and still lying quietly, he spoke clearly, without a trace of Alzheimer's disease in his voice. He said, "I'm doing just fine, Renée."

I'm a scientist, a physician—and pretty logical when it comes to constructs like heaven. We just don't know what happens when we die. There is no scientific, reproducible evidence. I was brought up in the Christian faith, and as a child heard all the usual stories of heaven—the pearly gates and Saint Peter with the judgment book in hand, ready to tell me if I was to be admitted. As a child, I imagined a ledger of all the good things and all the bad things that I had done. If the good outweighed the bad, Peter would let me in. As I grew older, I began to think that this black-and-white way of viewing the afterlife was too simplistic. It seemed designed to keep unruly children and wayward adults in check. In our early twenties, when we were dating, Harvey and I enjoyed long philosophical debates about such topics, and together we concluded that we would just never know for sure what happened after a person died.

All I knew for certain following Harvey's death was that his suffering was over. But when I awoke from the dream, I felt as if Harvey really had come back to tell me the message that he was well. The dream, even if it was just a construct in my brain, a meaningless figment of my desire, still gave me a sense of hope. To hear, from his own lips, that he had been restored to his true self, a highly intelligent and compassionate man, made my heart feel warm and expansive. I smiled as I remembered the dream. I shared it with our two daughters and prayed that they would have a dream or message of their own.

I dreamed of Harvey a second time, five years after his death. In this dream, I walked into my living room and was startled to see him there, walking toward the kitchen. He was young, healthy, and smiling, and not at all surprised to see me. I asked, "Harv, what are you doing here?" Nonchalantly, he replied, "I'm a necrologist." And that was all that transpired between us. Upon waking, I was confused by his answer and tried to understand it. I applied my Latin skills and decided that *necrologist* translated to "a person who studies death." *Well, that's interesting,* I thought. Even in the next realm, Harvey was studying his environment, observing, and almost certainly asking questions. I thought, *Maybe he now has all the answers to the questions we had about the afterlife, or at least is on the path of knowledge about it.*

But the most heartwarming realization that Harvey was still with us came in the form of a wise friend's words. I don't know why I didn't realize it myself, but the friend pointed out that Harvey was and is still physically present in our daughters, as half of their genetic makeup is from their father. One has his nose, the other his eyes. They both have his natural running ability. They both have his quiet disposition and have followed in his footsteps in professions that help others.

And now our oldest daughter has two young children of her own. These children inherited one-quarter of their genetic codes from the grandfather they will never meet, but we will teach them about this beloved man. We will tell them stories of their kind, beautiful, compassionate, strong, intelligent Grandpa Harvey. And he will live on, in full health and wholeness.

There are many joys to being a grandparent: watching your own child and their partner growing as parents, experiencing all the excitement without all the responsibility, and loving the new family with your whole being. But what really melts my heart is when Hazel and Micah, my grandchildren, call me by name, NayNay.

I picked out my grandma name when my first grandchild, Hazel, was yet to be born, as seems to be the norm these days. I wanted a name that reflected my given name, Renée, and was easy for a young child to say. I was fully receptive to being called something close to NayNay and decided I would accept whatever moniker she gave me. But Hazel called me NayNay very early on, right after she learned Dada and Mama. There might have been some coaching involved. And yes, it still melts my heart when she or her brother says my name excitedly when I come into their house or their room, or when either of them wants me to pick them up for a hug, or when I answer a FaceTime call, or when they are pointing to photographs of me.

They know my name. There is power in naming people. It confers personhood and recognition of the individual. One of the responsibilities of Adam and Eve in the Garden of Eden was to name all the animals. This story illustrates the power of naming. Humanity organizes the world by categorizing and putting labels on the creatures and their surroundings. Because this act cannot be reciprocal, due to our current understanding of animal communication, it also creates a hierarchy. Because we can name and label and categorize animals, and they cannot do the same to us, we have power over them.

So part of the charm of Hazel and Micah calling me by my name is that they are creating a world where they can name people and objects and gain a growing measure of control over their environment. They are learning to separate themselves and others from the whole. And though the hierarchy of parent or grandparent to child will hold for several more years, naming lays the foundation of reciprocity between us. When we see others as persons with names, it's harder to deny their humanity.

Before they could say my name, Hazel and Micah knew who I was—someone who loved and cared for them. I could see the light of recognition in their faces when they reached out for me. One of Harvey's last intelligible words was my name. After he lost that ability, he still knew who I was, though probably not what our specific relationship was. But he knew me as "his person." His whole being would light up when he saw me and reached out for me.

Eventually, Harvey lost all the light behind his eyes, the knowledge of his surroundings, even his own sense of self. He might have been deeply, deeply forgetful at this point, but I wasn't. I knew his name and what he meant to me, his family, his patients, and his friends. There might not have been any equality of intellect at that point, but I was still connecting to his soul through the shared memories that I continue to hold.

And we are sharing those memories with Hazel and Micah, as we teach them about Grandpa Harvey. In fact, their mother, our daughter Elena, has designated the anniversary of Harvey's death as Grandpa Harvey Day. It has turned a sad day of memories into a celebration of the man he was.

We also celebrate Harvey's legacy in other ways. On the Saturday before Thanksgiving, a little more than four years after he passed away, I gathered Harvey's ashes, my shovels, and a hoe; stopped at the garden shop to pick up an overcup oak sapling I'd purchased; then drove to our lake house to meet my daughters, their husbands, and my granddaughter. We would plant this tree at the lake using his ashes.

    I should back up a bit and tell you about the ashes. I had Harvey cremated immediately after his death. I should have made all the arrangements beforehand, but I didn't, so my daughters and I sat in the funeral home and made specific decisions about cremation the day after he passed away. When the ashes were ready, I brought them home. My father crafted a beautiful wooden box to hold them, and they sat in a closet because I couldn't think of a fitting location in which to scatter them. We did open the box when one of my daughters found someone who created jewelry with a scant amount of ashes. We three wear our rings every day.

    I should back up a bit and tell you about the plant nursery, Hanna's Garden Shop. It's located very near the first site of our family medicine practice. I can't recall what happened first, but either the owner and his family came to see us as patients or we visited Hanna's for shrubbery for our new house in 1992. In any event, the relationship continued for the duration of the existence of our medical practice. When the father passed away, the now-grown children inherited the shop. When I visited the garden shop to look for the oak tree that I wanted, I got to chat with one of the sons, reminding him of our families' long association and telling him of my plans for the tree.

    I should back up a bit and tell you about the tree I chose. For some reason, and I don't know why, but many years ago, Harvey began collecting acorns from a variety of oak called *overcup*. There must have been one in the neighborhood. Maybe the owner of Hanna's Garden Shop told him about this species with its acorn cup that almost completely encases the nut within. But one day I threw away his collection of overcup acorns, which were in a plastic baggie on our desk. I have a tendency to clean out unnecessary items—children's artwork, unused decorative napkins, duplicate kitchen tools—and I couldn't see the value of his collection. I know that I should have asked first. I have called myself the "Queen of Cull" and the "Princess of Purge," but that tendency can get me in trouble. This was one of those times. So I decided to redeem myself by planting this particular species of tree.

I should back up a bit and tell you why I chose my new lake house as the site to plant the overcup oak sapling. The lake house might seem like an odd location, since I purchased it long after Harvey passed away. He really would have loved this place, though. He grew up going to his grandparents' place on the lake and would recount stories of swimming, skiing, and fishing during his summers there, and he always longed for a similar experience for our daughters. We just never got around to it.

So we did indeed plant an overcup oak at the lake, using most of Harvey's ashes to mix with the soil the weekend before Thanksgiving. I kept about a third to stay with me in my home.

When we returned to the lake in late March, even though all the other trees in the area were coming back to life, Harvey's tree appeared to be dead. There had been a long period of freezing temperatures in December that had actually killed a lot of the plants at my home, so I wasn't surprised, just disappointed. When we returned in April, though, Harvey's tree was sporting new leaves. It was alive after all.

Later that summer, one of my sons-in-law noticed that Harvey's tree had been gnawed down and was just a twig sticking out of the ground. The tree had flourished over the summer, but evidently, a beaver or some other creature coveted it and took it for its own needs. I thought that I would buy a new sapling, plant it, and erect a small wire fence around it to protect it.

However, a few weeks later, the tree had sprouted numerous shoots from the chewed-off stub. I decided to leave the tiny stump with its new saplings, but still add the little wire fencing. The sun, rainwater, and ash-laden soil will bring forth a new tree. It all seems rather symbolic of Harvey's life, cut short, but continuing to put forth new versions of the original—our children and grandchildren, his legacy as a physician and friend.

Harvey's overcup oak will be with us now whenever we visit the lake, while celebrating holidays and birthdays, or when just sitting quietly on the porch watching the days unfold. As his tree grows, I will envision its branches as spreading love and protection over us.

❋❋❋

My challenges are not necessarily your challenges, but there are some commonalities in all of life's difficult times. They offer us the opportunity to grow, to know ourselves a bit better, and to eventually share what we've learned along the way. Challenging hikes have proven to be good metaphors for the challenges that arose for me. I learned from these hikes, as well as the plants and animals—including the humans—that I encountered along the way.

These hikes and other adventures had a healing effect on me while I was caregiving, when I was grieving, and when I was processing both of these experiences. After emerging from the overwhelm that was grief and coming back into my life, I could look back over all that I and my family had been through and see what had transpired more clearly than ever. You can't really see where you're going when you are in the midst of a storm. But after the fog of that period of my life had lifted, I could feel a resurgence of my lifeblood, and new horizons were visible.

And I began to learn that I was making meaning from Harvey's life, illness, and death. By remembering his life with more love in my heart than sadness, I realized that I was healing. Writing *Surfing the Waves of Alzheimer's* and weekly blog posts, speaking at conferences for Alzheimer's caregivers, and creating new traditions to honor him all added to the knowledge that I was moving forward. Grandchildren, more travel and adventure, and new writing projects confirm that notion for me still.

CONCLUSION

The Mountains We Climb

It took five days for our group of eight Kilimanjaro trekkers and forty porters to reach the last camp before the summit. We arrived at Kosovo Camp in the late afternoon. Camp was dreary and cold when we arrived, but the porters sang and danced us into the warmth of their hospitality. Dinner was early, about 5:30 p.m., then we went to bed, theoretically to sleep. As I lay in my tent, hunkered down in my zero-degree-rated sleeping bag, I rested. The patter of rain, then the louder smatter of sleet serenaded my attempt to sleep.

The wake-up call came at 11:00 p.m., with "breakfast" at 11:30, and we were on the trail at midnight. In that thirty-minute window between rousing and breakfast, I donned four layers of clothing, plus a good pair of insulated gloves and waterproof mittens. My head was adorned with a fleece balaclava, a wool beanie, and the hoods from my puffer coat and rain jacket. And a headlamp. I emerged into a bleak landscape of charcoal sky, volcanic boulders, and a dusting of snow. Even though I was bundled up, I could tell it was frigid, though I wasn't cold. I had no thermometer and no way to know what the temperature truly was, though.

The trail was narrow and consisted of numerous small switchbacks snaking three miles and three thousand feet of elevation up the mountain. I noticed that our group was being accompanied by more than the usual number of guides, but I didn't pay it much attention, as all my concentration was focused on putting one foot in front of the other, my headlamp illuminating each slow, short step. I certainly tried to employ all three of the techniques I'd learned on my travels—the mountaineer's rest step, pole pole pace, and the pressure breath. But nothing could alleviate the fatigue and windedness that set in pretty quickly for me.

We had scheduled breaks of five to ten minutes every forty-five or sixty minutes. These breaks were for sipping water and eating a snack—difficult tasks when heavily clothed and gloved, so the porters helped us take off our packs and gloves to access what we needed. As we climbed higher and the temperature fell further, the water in the tubing of our water bladder systems froze. We had been told this would happen, so we also carried Nalgene bottles of water. These were stored upside down so that ice would form on the surface nearer the bottom. Turning the bottle right side up broke up the thin layer of ice and created a crunchy, slushy, icy drink of water.

At our very first break, Nazareth, one of the porters who had joined us, came up to me and quietly offered, "Let me take your pack, Mama."

I looked up at him and replied, "Thank you, but I've got it. It's not that heavy."

He replied, "You are struggling, Mama. If I carry your pack, it will be easier for you." I gave him my backpack.

Nazareth periodically would place a hand lightly in the center of my back and murmur, "You are strong, Mama. You can do this. We will do it together, Mama." Just when I felt that I was too tired to continue, his reassuring words would call me back to the task.

As we continued up the mountain, I noticed each person in our group had their backpacks shouldered by other porters. They gave us our water, holding the containers to our lips if necessary. They unwrapped our snacks or helped us take off our gloves for us to do it ourselves. They massaged our shoulders. And incredibly, they called to each other in song, singing all the way up. I even took a cue from that and sang songs to myself that reminded me of my family in order to buoy my spirits.

I remember someone calling out that it was 4:00 a.m. We had been admonished not to look up to the summit, as it might deflate us to see how far we had yet to go. However, hearing that we were more than halfway there made me realize the goal was possible.

When we reached Stella Point at 6:00 a.m.—sunrise—I was spent. I sat down and tried to catch my breath. Everyone else in our group was jubilant and hugging and laughing, but I was in a dazed fog for a long minute until a porter delivered hot tea that revived me enough to join in the celebrations. Once revived, I took in the harsh, arctic, otherworldly landscape of snow topping barren rocks. In contrast, the sun now peeked through layers of gray clouds to shine a brilliant orange.

But this was not the summit. Stella Point was the end of the long, steep climb, reaching the rim of the crater of the volcano that is Kilimanjaro. It took another hour to reach Uhuru Peak, the true summit. Along the way there were massive glaciers and strange ice formations. My head and body were still exhausted, and my breathing was labored, but the end was in my sights now.

At Uhuru Peak, at just over nineteen thousand feet elevation, I surprised myself by crying joyful tears and hugging all our group members, Nazareth, and the other support team. We took photos, then quickly departed. Some in our group had started to experience signs of altitude sickness, and only a descent would reverse that. My breathlessness was a result of the altitude, but I had no other symptoms, and even that left me pretty quickly as I made my way down.

This was the hardest, most physically challenging experience I have ever had. I am proud of myself and of our group. Relying on the mountaineer's rest step, pole pole pace, and the pressure breath were all instrumental in making the ascent as easy as it could be. But it doesn't take anything away from our individual achievements to acknowledge that we couldn't have done it without all the support of each member of our group, our leaders, our guides, and the army of porters. What a reminder that no person is an island. We need each other. We thrive in the company of others. We can reach new heights when we work to support one another. Mountains can be conquered when we rely on our fellow life-travelers.

We use the expression "mountaintop experience" to convey the elation and exultation over a particularly astounding event. When we have these experiences, we feel breathless, our hearts race, and we feel on top of the world. From this vantage point, we can see the depths from which we have climbed, the valleys we ascended. If it's a clear day on the mountaintop, it feels like we can see the whole world spread out at our feet—all the questions are answered. We also can see, much more clearly, the other mountaintops in the range and the valleys we would have to cross to get there. Sometimes these mountaintop experiences just happen to us, without effort, but the more meaningful ones are the ones we have to work for.

And just as often as we talk of mountaintop experiences, that phrase is often followed by the acknowledgment "but one cannot stay on the mountaintop forever." There will always be other mountains we need to climb. The experience of climbing one mountain gives us the assurance that we have the strength to keep on climbing the next ones as they present themselves.

If we are vulnerable and allow others to see us struggling to ascend our personal mountains, we can be a source of confidence for their own next climb. "I could never do that" turns into "If she can do it, then maybe I can too." And once we have summited, and gained a new perspective of that mountain, we are better able to share what we learned along the way.

Now that's a whole lot of metaphor, the language in which I most easily speak, but what are your specific examples? Because I'm not really just talking about climbing actual mountains. What is your mountain? Did it just appear in front of you one day, or did you intentionally seek it out? What training have you had to do? What are your personal strengths that you can rely on? What fears are holding you back? Can self-compassion assist you in your climb? What in you needs a new perspective, an adaptation, or a complete overhaul? Who do you look to for inspiration on how to get to the summit? Who can help with the itinerary of your climb? Who will be there to assist you? Can you ask for help?

What future mountain is calling you back home to your true self, the god-spark within?

***

I have climbed the mountain of Harvey's terminal illness and the aftermath of grief. I've shed the skin of old ways of viewing my life. I've cocooned in the safety of my family, escaped into a smaller hideaway cottage, then expanded that hearth. That cocooning allowed me to morph into a new iteration of myself. No longer wife or physician, I am a new creature with crimped wings that are still unfurling. I am learning to fly solo. And if you see me, or read my words, or hear me speak, I pray that you see the butterfly that I hope I am becoming.

Instead of marveling at the beauty of the butterfly, I hope that you see the deep meaning I've come to appreciate in this new life. The legacy of Harvey's life, and our life together, before and during his time with dementia, is memorialized in my first memoir. This second book of stories and essays gleaned from hiking, nature, and travel during the time after his death is testimony that life can be lived and experienced afresh. My hope is that you, too, can acknowledge your own inner voice, embrace change, walk in community, and have the courage to live a life of authenticity, abundance, curiosity, and joy.

My story will continue as I learn and grow, encountering more of what life has to teach me. I know that I have been changed, but not defined, by those passages. Maybe along the way I even reclaimed parts of that god-spark with which I was born by opening myself to being more mindfully present and aware. I call that god-spark, that child that lives inside of me, "the dancing girl." It may be partly literal, but I also see her as the joy-filled child who looked at the world in wonder, playing and dancing in the present moments. My parents tell me that I was a very happy child. Somewhere along the way, I became serious, realizing that I garnered more accolades for my scholarship, studiousness, and playing by the rules. The dancing girl still danced occasionally, but she danced less and less often as her responsibilities overtook her. She could still dance as she played the piano or created in her studio or took walks in the woods. But there was too much to attend to. Too many people that depended on her, her calendar bursting with to-do lists.

By taking the pause that grief, then retirement, and then the Covid pandemic enforced, the dancing girl began to re-emerge. She traveled via different vehicles to locations near and far. She walked on trails in forests and on mountains around the world. And she kept her eyes open for what lessons the world could teach her. Journaling became a way for her to process what she was experiencing, both during her husband's decline as well as after. And once she had found her balance again, she shared what she had learned, and was still learning, with her community—a community of caregivers and fellow travelers in the world.

And she danced and twirled and glided down the path of the rest of her life. Sometimes she even put away her map and trusted her instincts. And she found her way back home to herself. Again. And again.

Acknowledgments

The amount of time and energy it takes to birth a book into the world was wildly underestimated by this writer, even though this is a second book. My first memoir, *Surfing the Waves of Alzheimer's*, seemed to write itself. It took just four months to write, and at the end of that time, I felt like I had a finished product that just needed polishing before I released it into the world.

This second memoir was laborious in unexpected ways. Most of the material had already been written and published on my website as blog posts, and I thought it would be an easy thing to assemble the best of these short essays and group them by categories. Once I had done that, I searched for a professional content editor to read this first-draft manuscript. I was humbled to realize that my attempt at corralling my short essays into a coherent whole was essentially a mess. My editor, Audra Figgins, kindly suggested ways to better structure the whole so that it could focus on themes rather than my original grouping by subject. Her ideas spurred me to shake up the entire thing and wrestle it into some coherent shape. We landed on the hero's journey as a likely structure, and because I had just returned from a pilgrimage to Greece where our group of pilgrims studied Odysseus's adventures, this felt just right. Later travels to Mount Kilimanjaro added to the themes that were taking place in the whole.

I am indebted to an eclectic group of cheerleaders who

encouraged me to pursue this book: Dehryl and Sonja, Kathy and Hanna, Anna and other Beacon writers, Nan and Gladys, Mary Evelyn and Javacia, Audrey, Jill, and the other Heady Tormentors. When I put out a call for beta readers to my three hundred subscribers, two former patients and a distant friend responded almost immediately. Thank you all for your support as I seemed to fiddle with this manuscript for endless months.

To my family of origin, my family of choice, and the little family that Harvey and I created—thank you all for your unwavering love and encouragement.

To the audiences of caregivers who have listened to my stories, asked questions, and shared your own stories with me—you are seen, you are amazing, you are loved.

Resources

Books

On Death and Dying: What the Dying Have to Teach Doctors, Nurses, Clergy and Their Own Families, Elisabeth Kübler-Ross, MD, Scribner, reissue edition, August 12, 2014.
Ambiguous Loss: Learning to Live with Unresolved Grief, Pauline Boss, Harvard University Press, October 2, 2000.
Finding Meaning: The Sixth Stage of Grief, David Kessler, Simon and Schuster, Scribner imprint, November 5, 2019.
Chicken Soup for the Soul: Navigating Eldercare & Dementia, editor-in-chief Amy Newmark, Chicken Soup for the Soul, June 22, 2021.
Before the Diagnosis: Stories of Life and Love Before Dementia, edited by Gincy Heins, February 25, 2018.
Before the Diagnosis: More Stories of Life and Love Before Dementia, edited by Gincy Heins, March 27, 2022.
Braiding Sweetgrass: Indigenous Wisdom, Scientific Knowledge, and the Teachings of Plants, Robin Wall Kimmerer, Milkweed Editions, August 11, 2015.
The Hidden Life of Trees: What They Feel, How They Communicate—Discoveries from a Secret World, Peter Wohlleben, Greystone Books, September 13, 2016.
Enchanted by Daphne: The Life of an Evolutionary Naturalist, Peter R. Grant, Princeton University Press, May 23, 2023.
Surfing the Waves of Alzheimer's: Principles of Caregiving That

Kept Me Upright, Renée Brown Harmon, MD, Many Hats Publishing, September 7, 2020.

The 36-Hour Day: A Family Guide to Caring for People Who Have Alzheimer Disease and Other Dementias, Nancy L. Mace and Peter V. Rabins, Johns Hopkins Press Health Book, 7th edition, August 10, 2021.

Ten Thousand Joys and Ten Thousand Sorrows: A Couple's Journey Through Alzheimer's, Olivia Ames Hoblitzelle, Tarcher, September 30, 2010.

Learning to Speak Alzheimer's: A Groundbreaking Approach for Everyone Dealing with the Disease, Joanne Koenig Coste, Harper Paperbacks, September 8, 2004.

Loving Someone Who Has Dementia: How to Find Hope while Coping with Stress and Grief, Pauline Boss, Jossey-Bass, August 9, 2011.

Bible sources: Matthew 8:23–27, Mark 4:35–41, and Luke 8:22–25.

Websites

https://www.alltrails.com/
https://www.talkspace.com/blog/types-of-grief/
https://www.ncbi.nlm.nih.gov/pmc/articles/PMC6228869/
https://www.nytimes.com/2023/08/23/health/ptsd-writing-therapy.html#:~:text=The%20treatment%2C%20called%20written%20exposure,event%20has%20affected%20their%20lives
https://www.becomingwhoyouare.net/paper-versus-digital-journaling-which-one-is-better/
https://www.veriditas.org/

https://www.fs.usda.gov/wildflowers/beauty/lichens/about
.shtml#:~:text=Lichens%20are%20a%20complex%20
life,shape%20to%20its%20fruiting%20bodies
https://askabiologist.asu.edu/content/ant-factoids
https://www.pbs.org/newshour/science/ants-move
-really-big-stuff
https://www.blueskytrekking.com/
https://www.mindful.org/the-science-of-gratitude/
https://www.barefootsoulswellness.com/swiss-alps
-adventure.html
https://www.radiantnursing.com/blog/dementia-evaluation
https://tailofthedragon.com/
https://www.health.harvard.edu/healthbeat/learning
-diaphragmatic-breathing
https://www.rmiguides.com/blog/2014/07/07
/mountaineering_training_moving_air_breathing
_for_performance#:~:text=Pressure%20breathing%20
is%20a%20technique%20nearly%20all,just%20a%20
derivative%20of%20the%20belly%20breath.&text
=Essentially%20belly%20breathing%20with%20a%20
forceful%20exhale%2C,by%20increasing%20the%20
pressure%20in%20the%20lungs
https://www.healthline.com/health/box-breathing
https://www.alabamaforeverwild.com/sipsey-river-complex
https://pura-aventura.com/us/travel-stories/why-animals
-in-galapaogs-islands-are-fearless
https://www.fs.usda.gov/wildflowers/beauty/columbines
/birdsandbees.shtml
https://news.harvard.edu/gazette/story/2018/02/harvard
-researchers-study-flower-that-catapults-pollen/
https://en.wikipedia.org/wiki/Charles_Darwin
  (This long article on Wikipedia is well researched and
  documented.)

https://www.wildlifewatch.org.uk/what-happens-inside-chrysalis#:~:text=A%20butterfly's%20lifecycle%20has%20four,its%20body%20from%2
https://www.fs.usda.gov/wildflowers/pollinators/Monarch_Butterfly/index.shtml
https://www.allaboutbirds.org/guide/Double-crested_Cormorant/overview
https://animals.sandiegozoo.org/animals/galapagos-tortoise
https://www.philcousineau.net/
https://blackbirdguides.com/blogs/alpine-climbing/mountaineering-fundamentals-the-rest-step
https://www.nwf.org/Educational-Resources/Wildlife-Guide/Plants-and-Fungi/Resurrection-Fern
https://alzauthors.com/
(This is an invaluable resource to caregivers of persons living with any form of dementia. It includes a compilation of books, blogs, podcasts, and videos from a broad range of creators.)

Articles

Parts of chapter 5, "Time Travel," were originally published in Reckon News, January 20, 2021: https://www.reckon.news/honey/2021/01/from-life-mate-to-playmate-how-alzheimers-transformed-my-marriage.html

About the Author

After retiring from a thirty-year career as a family medicine physician, Renée Brown Harmon, MD, published *Surfing the Waves of Alzheimer's: Principles of Caregiving That Kept Me Upright* in 2020, a teaching memoir about her late husband's time with younger-onset Alzheimer's disease. She lives in Birmingham, Alabama, and *Life Hikes* is her second book.

www.ingramcontent.com/pod-product-compliance
Lightning Source LLC
Chambersburg PA
CBHW060607080526
44585CB00013B/725